GOD'S PSYCHIATRY

D1008021

CHARLES L. ALLEN

FLEMING H. REVELL COMPANY
Old Tappan, New Jersey

To my father

THE LATE REVEREND J. R. ALLEN

and to my mother

LULA FRANKLIN ALLEN

CONTENTS

PART III: HOW TO TALK TO GOD

THE LORD'S PRAYER

PART IV: THE KEYS TO THE KINGDOM

THE BEATITUDES

THE HEALING OF MIND AND SOUL

OUR MODERN WORD "PSYCHIATRY" COMES FROM THE TWO Greek words Ψυχή (*psyche*) and ιατρεία (*iatreia*): *psyche-iatreia*. The word "psyche" really means the person, and is variously translated as "breath," "soul," "mind," "reason," and the like.

The word *iatreia* means "treatment," "healing," "restoring," and the like.

So, put the two words together and we have "the healing of the mind," or, as David might have said, "the restoring of the soul."

The word can mean medical treatment, or the treatment by a physician, but that is only one of its meanings, and I feel that the science of psychiatry is not to be limited to the medical profession. Often the minister is a psychiatrist, because he deals not only with the minds of people but also with their souls.

In fact, the very essence of religion is to adjust the mind and soul of man, and we have long ago learned, as in this book I quote Augustine as saying, "My soul is restless until it finds its rest in Thee, O God." Healing means bringing the person into a right relationship with the physical, mental and spiritual laws of God.

The physician is a minister of God. All true scientific research is merely an organized effort to learn the laws of God and how they operate.

7

The teacher is also a minister of God. The teacher seeks to train the mind, to seek truth and know truth when it is found. A mind which thinks error is a sick mind. So a teacher is practicing part of the great science of psychiatry.

Beyond our bodies and minds are our souls. The minister is concerned with man's soul; he believes that if his soul is sick the man is sick, indeed. And only God can heal the soul.

So, the first and most important psychiatry must be God's psychiatry, the essence of which I find contained in the four best known passages of The Bible: The Twenty-Third Psalm, The Ten Commandments, The Lord's Prayer, and The Beatitudes.

As the pastor of a church located on a main thoroughfare in Atlanta, it has been my privilege to counsel with many people who needed help. As a result of writing a daily column for *The Atlanta Constitution* and speaking regularly for some years over WSB radio and WSB-TV, my mail has brought me many letters from people telling me of their problems. I have not yet found one in need of the healing of his or her mind or situation where I have not also found that somewhere back down the line in that life one of the basic principles that I write about in this book was violated. So I say that most of all we need God's Psychiatry.

In this small volume I have not concerned myself so much with cases or techniques as I did in two earlier books—*Roads to Radiant Living* and *In Quest of God's Power*. Instead, I have sought here to explain the great principles that God has ordained to govern the life of man, believing, as I do, that if man lives according to these principles, his life will be whole and healthy. If he violates them, he will be sick. As someone has put it:

> *He who formed our frame,*
> *Made man a perfect whole;*
> *And made the body's health*
> *Depend upon the soul.*

There are many to whom I would like to express deep appreciation. To the members of the Grace Methodist Church in Atlanta, whose love and loyal support are far greater than I deserve; to my secretary, Mrs. Charles T. Moss, who not only is efficient but also is kind and understanding and loyal; to my assistant, Miss Mary Hogan, who daily does much work that I should be doing and thereby allows me more time for my study and speaking engagements; to my lovely wife, Leila, who continues to love me, though I give so much of my time to my work and to other people.

C. L. A.

Grace Methodist Church
458 Ponce de Leon Avenue, N.E.
Atlanta, Ga.

PUBLISHER'S NOTE

Dr. Allen is now minister of the First Methodist Church, Houston, Texas.

PART I

HOW TO THINK OF GOD

The Twenty-third Psalm

The Lord is my shepherd: I shall
not want.

He maketh me to lie down in green
pastures; he leadeth me beside the still
waters.

He restoreth my soul: he leadeth me
in the paths of righteousness for his
name's sake.

Yea, though I walk through the valley
of the shadow of death, I will fear no
evil: for thou art with me; thy rod and
staff they comfort me.

Thou preparest a table before me in
the presence of mine enemies: thou
anointest my head with oil; my cup runneth
over.

Surely goodness and mercy shall follow
me all the days of my life: and I will
dwell in the house of the Lord for ever.

1. A PATTERN OF THINKING

A MAN I ADMIRE VERY MUCH CAME IN TO SEE ME. MANY years ago he started with his company at the bottom but with determination to get to the top. He has unusual abilities and energy and he used all he had. Today he is president of his company and he has all the things that go with his position.

Yet, along the way, he left out something, and one of the things he did not achieve is happiness. He was a nervous, tense, worried, and sick man. Finally, one of his physicians suggested that he talk with a minister.

We talked of how his physicians had given him prescriptions and he had taken them. Then I took a sheet of paper and wrote out my prescription for him. I prescribed the Twenty-third Psalm, five times a day for seven days.

I insisted that he take it just as I prescribed. He was to read it the first thing when he awakened in the morning. Read it carefully, meditatively, and prayerfully. Immediately after breakfast, he was to do exactly the same thing. Also immediately after lunch, again after dinner, and, finally, the last thing before he went to bed.

It was not to be a quick, hurried reading. He was to think about each phrase, giving his mind time to soak up as much of the meaning as possible. At the end of just one week, I promised, things would be different for him.

That prescription sounds simple, but really it isn't. The Twenty-third Psalm is one of the most powerful pieces of writing in existence, and it can do marvelous things for any person. I have suggested this to many people and in every instance which I know of it being tried it has produced results. It can change your life in seven days.

One man told me that he did not have time to be bothered with reading it during the day, so he just read it five times in the morning. However, when a physician prescribed a medicine after each meal, or every certain number of hours, no right thinking person would take the full day's dose at one time.

Some have told me that after two or three days they felt they knew it sufficiently, and thus, instead of taking time to read it thoughtfully, they would just think about it through the day. That won't work. To be most effective, it must be taken exactly as prescribed.

Ralph Waldo Emerson said, "A man is what he thinks about all day long." Marcus Aurelius said, "A man's life is what his thoughts make it." Norman Vincent Peale says, "Change your thoughts and you change your world." The Bible says, "For as he thinketh in his heart, so is he" (Proverbs 23:7).

The Twenty-third Psalm is a pattern of thinking, and when a mind becomes saturated with it, a new way of thinking and a new life are the result. It contains only 118 words. One could memorize it in a short time. In fact, most of us already know it. But its power is not in memorizing the words, but rather in thinking the thoughts.

The power of this Psalm lies in the fact that it represents a positive, hopeful, faith approach to life. We assume it was written by David, the same David who had a black chapter of sin and failure in his life. But he spends no time in useless regret and morbid looking back.

David possesses the same spirit that St. Paul expresses: "Forgetting those things which are behind, and reaching forth unto those things which are before, I press toward the mark" (Philippians 3:13), or the spirit of our Lord when He said, "Neither do I condemn thee; go and sin no more" (John 8:11).

Take it as I prescribe, and in seven days a powerful new way of thinking will be deeply and firmly implanted within your mind that will bring marvelous changes in your thinking and give you a new life.

2. THE LORD IS MY SHEPHERD; I SHALL NOT WANT

IMMEDIATELY AFTER WORLD WAR II THE ALLIED ARMIES gathered up many hungry, homeless children and placed them in large camps. There the children were abundantly fed and cared for. However, at night they did not sleep well. They seemed restless and afraid.

Finally, a psychologist hit on a solution. After the children were put to bed, they each received a slice of bread to hold. If they wanted more to eat, more was provided, but this particular slice was not to be eaten—it was just to hold.

The slice of bread produced marvelous results. The

child would go to sleep, subconsciously feeling it would have something to eat tomorrow. That assurance gave the child a calm and peaceful rest.

In the Twenty-third Psalm, David points out something of the same feeling in the sheep when he says, "The Lord is my shepherd; I shall not want." Instinctively, the sheep knows the shepherd has made plans for its grazing tomorrow. He knows the shepherd made ample provision for it today, so will he tomorrow, so the sheep lies down in its fold with, figuratively speaking, the piece of bread in its hand.

So this Psalm does not begin with a petition asking God for something, rather it is a calm statement of fact—"The Lord *is* my shepherd." We do not have to beg God for things.

As Roy L. Smith and others have pointed out, God made provision for our needs long before we even had a need. Before we ever felt cold, God began storing up oil, coal, and gas to keep us warm. He knew we would be hungry, so, even before He put man on the earth, God put fertility into the soil and life into the seeds. "Your father knoweth what things ye have need of, before ye ask him," said Jesus (Matthew 6:8).

The greatest source of human worry is about tomorrow, as it was with the women going to the tomb of Jesus Easter morning. They missed the beauty of the early morning sun and the glory of the flowers along the way. They were worrying about who would roll away the stone. And when they got there it was already rolled away.

In another place (Psalm 37:25) David says, "I have been young, and now am old: yet have I not seen the righteous forsaken, nor his seed begging bread." Come to think about it, neither have I. Have you?

All life came from God. That includes my life. God keeps faith with fowls of the air and the grass of the field. And Jesus asks us to think that if God will do so much for a simple bird or a wild flower, how much more will He do for us (Matthew 6:25,34).

St. Paul says, "My God shall supply all your needs" (Philippians 4:19). David puts it, "The Lord is my shepherd, I shall not want." With that faith we can work today without worrying about tomorrow.

3. HE MAKETH ME TO LIE DOWN IN GREEN PASTURES

ONE MORNING AS I WAS HURRIEDLY DRESSING TO BEGIN A full and thrilling day I felt a pain in my back. I mentioned it to my wife but was sure it would soon pass away. However, she insisted I see a physician, and he put me in a hospital.

In the hospital I was very unhappy. I had no time to be wasting there in bed. My calendar was full of good activities and the doctor had told me to cancel all my appointments for at least a month. A dear minister friend of mine came to see me. He sat down and very firmly said, "Charles, I have only one thing to say to you—'He *maketh* me to lie down.'"

I lay there thinking about those words in the Twenty-third Psalm long after my friend had gone. I thought about how the shepherd starts the sheep grazing about

4 o'clock in the morning. The sheep walk steadily as they graze; they are never still.

By 10 o'clock, the sun is beaming down and the sheep are hot, tired, and thirsty. The wise shepherd knows that the sheep must not drink when it is hot, neither when its stomach is filled with undigested grass.

So the shepherd makes the sheep lie down in green pastures, in a cool, soft spot. The sheep will not eat lying down, so he chews his cud, which is nature's way of digestion.

Study the lives of great people, and you will find every one of them drew apart from the hurry of life for rest and reflection. Great poems are not written on crowded streets, lovely songs are not written in the midst of clamoring multitudes; our visions of God come when we stop. The Psalmist said, "Be still, and know that I am God" (Psalm 46:10).

Elijah found God, not in the earthquake or the fire, but in "a still small voice." Moses saw the burning bush as he was out on the hillside. Saul of Tarsus was on the lonely, quiet road to Damascus when he saw the heavenly vision. Jesus took time to be alone and to pray.

This is perhaps the most difficult thing for us to do. We will work for the Lord, we will sing, preach, teach. We will even suffer and sacrifice. Lustily we sing, "Work, for the night is coming," "Onward, Christian soldiers," "Stand up, stand up for Jesus."

We sometimes forget that before Jesus sent out His disciples to conquer the world, He told them to tarry for prayer and the power of God.

Sometimes God puts us on our backs in order to give us a chance to look up: "He maketh me to lie down."

Many times we are forced, not by God, but by circumstances of one sort or another to lie down. That can always be a blessed experience. Even the bed of an invalid may be a blessing if he takes advantage of it!

> *Take from our souls the strain and stress,*
> *And let our ordered lives confess—*
> *The beauty of Thy peace.*

> —WHITTIER

4. HE LEADETH ME BESIDE THE STILL WATERS

THE SHEEP IS A VERY TIMID CREATURE. ESPECIALLY IS IT afraid of swiftly moving water, which it has good reason to fear.

The sheep is a very poor swimmer because of its heavy coat of wool. It would be like a man trying to swim with his overcoat on. The water soaks into the sheep's coat and pulls it down.

Instinctively, the sheep knows it cannot swim in swift current. The sheep will not drink from a moving stream. The sheep will drink only from still waters.

The shepherd does not laugh at the sheep's fears. He does not try to force the sheep. Instead, as he leads his sheep across the mountains and valleys, he is constantly on the watch for still waters, where the thirst of the sheep may be quenched.

If there are no still waters available, while the sheep are resting, the shepherd will gather up stones to fashion a dam across a small stream to form a pool from which even the tiniest lamb may drink without fear.

This petition of the Twenty-third Psalm has wonderful meaning for us. God knows our limitations, and He does not condemn us because we have weaknesses. He does not force us where we cannot safely and happily go. God never demands of us work which is beyond our strength and abilities.

Instead, God is constantly ministering to our needs. He understands the loads upon our shoulders. He also knows where the places of nourishment and refreshment are located.

It gives one confidence to know that even while he is sleeping, the Shepherd is working to prepare for his needs tomorrow.

We are told, "He will not suffer thy foot to be moved: he that keepeth thee will not slumber. Behold, he that keepeth Israel shall neither slumber nor sleep" (Psalm 121:3,4).

One of the finest ways to relieve a tension in your life is to picture still water clearly in your mind. Maybe a little lake nestling among some pines. Maybe a tiny, cool spring on some hillside. Maybe a calm sea with gentle, rippling waves.

After the picture becomes clear, then start repeating and believing, "He leadeth me beside the still waters." Such an experience produces a marvelous surrender and trust that enables one to face the heat of the day confidently, knowing there is refreshing and relaxed power awaiting under the leadership of one wiser than we.

The great Martin Luther used to sing:

> *A mighty fortress is our God,*
> *A bulwark never failing:*
> *Our helper He, amidst the flood*
> *Of mortal ills prevailing.*

That is the feeling David had when he wrote the Twenty-third Psalm.

As this Psalm saturates your mind it gives you that same assurance, too.

5. HE RESTORETH MY SOUL

A LETTER TO ME CONCLUDES WITH: "LIFE ENDED FOR ME somewhere during these years . . . through a slow process. It took years to stifle my faith; but now it is entirely gone. . . . I am only a shell. Perhaps the shell . . . [is] gone."

I would like to talk with the writer of that letter about the meaning of David's words in the Twenty-third Psalm, "He restoreth my soul." David remembered that as the sheep start out in the morning to graze, each takes a definite place in line and holds that same position all during the day.

However, some time during the day each sheep leaves its place in line and trots over to the shepherd. The shepherd gently rubs the nose and ears, lightly scratches the ears, and whispers in an ear of the sheep. Reassured and encouraged, the sheep takes its place in line again.

David remembered how close he once was to God, how God protected him as he went out to meet the giant Goliath, how God guided him along the way to success. Then David got busy. He was able to look after himself. He felt no need of God.

David lost his nearness to God. He did wrong. He became unhappy. His burden of guilt became too heavy to bear. Then he repented. God heard, forgave, and restored. He became a new man.

The human mind is like the human body. It can be wounded. Sorrow is a wound. It cuts deeply, but sorrow is a clean wound, and will heal unless something gets into the wound, such as bitterness, self-pity, or resentment.

Wrong is also a wound.

When I violate my standards I wound my mind, and it is an unclean wound. Time will not heal that wound. Gradually, a sense of guilt can destroy a life and make it "only a shell." There is only one physician who can heal. The Fifty-first Psalm is the prayer David prayed.

"He restoreth my soul" can have another meaning. Moffatt translates it to read, "He revives life in me." Like a watch, the human spirit can just run down. We lose our drive and push. We become less willing to attempt the difficult. We are crusaders no longer.

Like squeezing the juice from an orange and leaving just the pulp, life has a way of squeezing the spirit out of a person. A person can become "only a shell." We feel the thrill of no new enthusiasm, the dawn of a new day leaves us cold and hopeless.

The Bible tells that God made the first man "and breathed into his nostrils the breath of life; and man became a living soul" (Genesis 2:7). And God has the power and the willingness to breathe a new breath of life into one who has lost.

Only God has the power. Speaking to a large number of physicians in Atlanta, Dr. R. B. Robins declared, "The psychiatrist's couch cannot take the place of the church in solving the problems of a frustrated society."

"He restoreth my soul"—"He revives life in me."

6. HE LEADETH ME IN THE PATHS OF RIGHTEOUSNESS FOR HIS NAME'S SAKE

ON A PLAQUE AT FLORIDA'S SINGING TOWER YOU CAN READ these words; "I come here to find myself. It is so easy to get lost in the world." That is true.

We come to the forks of life's road and cannot decide which way to turn. There are decisions to be made and yet it is so hard to decide. We do get lost. We need guidance, and confidently David in the Twenty-third Psalm declares, "He leadeth me in the paths of righteousness" (in the right paths).

Doubtless David remembers his own experiences as a shepherd. He knew that the sheep has no sense of direction. A dog, a cat, or a horse, if lost, can find its way back. They seem to have a compass within themselves. Not so with a sheep.

The sheep has very poor eyes. It cannot see ten or fifteen yards ahead. Palestinian fields were covered with narrow paths over which the shepherds led their sheep to pasture. Some of these paths led to a precipice over which the stupid sheep might fall to its death.

Other paths lead up a blind alley. But some paths lead to green pastures and still waters. The sheep followed the shepherd, knowing it was walking in the right path. Sometimes the shepherd led over steep and difficult places, but the paths he followed always ended up somewhere.

The sheep was willing to trust that "somewhere" to the shepherd's judgment. Even as we sing,

> Lord, I would place my hand in Thine,
> Nor ever murmur nor repine;
> Content, whatever lot I see,
> Since 'tis my God that leadeth me.

Perhaps David remembered his forefathers as they made their way across a trackless wilderness from Egypt to the Promised Land. God sent a pillar of fire by night and a pillar of cloud by day. Following it, the Israelites did come to the land they longed for.

For some the paths of righteousness means hard going at times. Dr. Ralph W. Sockman tells about an English lad who decided to join the army for service in India. When asked the reason for his choice, he said: "I hear that in the Indian army they pay you a lot for doing a little. When you get on further, they pay you more for doing less. When you retire, they pay you quite a lot for doing nothing."

Though God does not put a bed of roses on the battlefield or a carpet on the race track; though He does not promise us an easy, effortless life, He does promise us strength and He does promise to go with us.

Notice that the Psalm says, "He *leadeth* me." God doesn't drive. He is climbing the same hill that we climb— man is not alone. As we take life one step at a time, we can walk with Him the right paths.

The wise man says, "In all thy ways acknowledge him and he shall direct thy paths" (Proverbs 3:6). That is true. The person who sincerely seeks to do God's will, whatever His will may be, will know the leadership of Eternal Wisdom.

He will lead you to your Promised Land.

7. YEA, THOUGH I WALK THROUGH THE VALLEY OF THE SHADOW OF DEATH, I WILL FEAR NO EVIL: FOR THOU ART WITH ME

LET ME DRAW AN ILLUSTRATION FROM THE STORY OF A mother who collapsed when news came that her son had been killed. She went into her room, closed the door, and would see no one.

Her minister came and sat down by her bedside, but she would not speak to him. For a little while all was quiet and then slowly he began saying, "The Lord is my shepherd, I shall not want." Phrase by phrase, he gently spoke the words of the Psalm, and she listened.

When he came to that great phrase of comfort, she joined in and together they said, "Yea, though I walk through the valley of the shadow of death, I will fear no evil; for thou art with me."

A smile flickered on her lips, and she said, "I see it differently now."

Henry Ward Beecher says the Twenty-third Psalm is the nightingale of the Psalms. The nightingale sings its sweetest when the night is darkest. And for most of us death is the most terrifying fact of life.

After a funeral, someone said to me. "You conduct a lot of funerals; doesn't it become routine for you?" The answer is no. You never become accustomed to death. Each one is a new and fresh experience.

We bring our flowers and we have lovely music, but not even flowers and music can make a tomb a place of cheer. And death makes us afraid. We feel so helpless and alone.

Of course, "the valley of the shadow of death" refers to more than the actual experiences of physical death. It has been translated, "the glen of gloom." It might refer to every hard and terrifying experience of life.

The Basque Sheepherder describes an actual Valley of the Shadow of Death in Palestine. It leads from Jerusalem to the Dead Sea and is a very narrow and dangerous pathway through the mountain range. The path is rough, and there is danger that a sheep may fall at any moment to its death.

It is a forbidding journey that one dreads to take. But the sheep is not afraid. Why? Because the shepherd is with it.

And so come those dark places in life through which we are compelled to pass. Death is one. Disappointment is another. Loneliness is another. There are many more.

I have said to many people in "the valley of the

shadow" to get off by themselves in a quiet place. Quit struggling for a little while. Forget the many details. Stop your mind for a little while from hurrying on to the morrow and to next year and beyond.

Just stop, become still and quiet, and in the midst of your "glen of gloom" you will feel a strange and marvelous presence more powerfully than you have ever felt it before. Many have told me of feeling that presence—of hearing the nightingale sing in the darkness.

Wherever my pathway leads, I will not be afraid, said David, and countless multitudes also have rid themselves of fear. Why? "For thou art with me." There is power in His presence.

8. THY ROD AND THY STAFF THEY COMFORT ME

I ONCE KNEW A MAN WHO WAS HURT BADLY IN A CYCLONE. From then on much of the joy of life was gone for him. Not because of his injury, but rather because he was afraid that another cyclone might come. There was nothing he could do.

He worried because there was still nothing he would be able to do if he saw another cyclone coming—until one day his children decided to build a cyclone cellar. They completed it and the man looked at it with relaxed joy. Now, no matter how hard a cyclone blew, he had protection. It was a great comfort to him.

In the Twenty-third Psalm we read, "Thy rod and thy staff they comfort me." The sheep is a helpless animal. It has no weapon with which to fight. It is easy prey to any wild beast of the field. It is afraid.

But the shepherd carries a rod, which is a heavy, hard club two to three feet long. When David wrote this Psalm he probably remembered his own need for such a rod. In I Samuel 17, David tells Saul how he slew a lion and a bear in protecting his sheep.

Also, the shepherd carried a staff, which was about eight feet long. The end of the staff was turned into a crook. Many paths in Palestine were along the steep sides of mountains. The sheep would lose its footing and slip down, hanging helplessly on some ledge below.

With his staff the shepherd could reach down, place the crook over the small chest of the sheep and lift it back onto the pathway. The sheep instinctively is comforted by the shepherd's rod and staff.

It is the comfort of knowing that the shepherd will be able to meet an emergency.

I have insurance on my automobile. I hope I will never need it, but I am comforted by the fact that I do have it.

I regret that my country finds it necessary to spend so much money on military preparedness. Yet, when I think of the condition of the world, my country's strength comforts me.

There are needs of my life that I cannot meet, and, like St. Paul it comforts me to say, "Now unto him that is able to do exceeding abundantly above all that we ask or think" (Ephesians 3:20).

Seemingly there is overwhelming evil in the world.

We are a scared people. Many times we feel helpless; then we find comfort in realizing the power of God.

Certainly I do not think of God as just a cyclone cellar or an insurance policy. Yet I can say with James Montgomery:

God is my salvation: what foe have I to fear?
In darkness and temptation, my light, my help is near:
Though hosts encamp around me, firm in the fight I stand,
What terror can confound me, with God at my right hand?

"Thy rod and thy staff"—that takes a lot of the dread and fear of the future out of my heart.

9. *THOU PREPAREST A TABLE BEFORE ME IN THE PRESENCE OF MINE ENEMIES*

IN ONE TOWN WHERE WE LIVED THERE AROSE AN ISSUE OVER whether or not a poolroom should be permitted to open. My father vigorously crusaded against it, and I remember someone rather jokingly asked him if he thought he would be tempted to play pool.

He said no, but that he had some boys and he did not want his boys in a poolroom. He might have kept his boys away, but he felt it would be safer to keep the poolroom away. My father's feeling in the matter serves to illustrate what David meant in the Twenty-third Psalm when he said: "Thou preparest a table before me in the presence of mine enemies."

In the pastures of the Holy Land grew poisonous plants which were fatal to the sheep if eaten. Also, there were plants whose sharp thorns would penetrate the soft noses of the sheep and cause ugly sores.

Each spring the shepherd would take his mattock and dig out these enemies of the sheep, pile them up and burn them. Thus the pastures were safe for the sheep to graze. The pasture became, as it were, a table prepared. The present enemies were destroyed.

We constantly must do this for our children. When my children go and come from school, a police woman stands on the corner. She is there to protect my children.

Happily, in Atlanta our school children have not yet been faced with a serious dope situation. But I want my city to keep it that way, exercising all possible vigilance. I feel the same way about obscene literature and many other things that harm and destroy life. We must constantly crusade against the enemies of life.

It is not enough for the farmer to plant his seed. He must go through his crop again and again to destroy the weeds. So must the spirit of God in man militantly crusade. It is not enough just to preach the Gospel. We must destroy the enemies.

Recently my children were vaccinated against some disease. I thank medical science for going before to prevent or destroy the cause of the disease. Parents, scientists, government, society as a whole, must prepare a table, destroying the enemies, so that all good life may be safely nourished.

After a sermon on race prejudice, a good man took me to task for not preaching the Gospel. But I have seen prejudice and false ideas of racial superiority destroy the opportunities for children of God. I feel my sermon was a compulsory part of the Gospel.

It is not enough just piously to sit around being good. There are times when "the Son of God goes forth to war."

One other thought—Jesus expresses the petition of David when He prays, "Lead us not into temptation." As we move along through life, we know there will be enemies seeking to destroy. Many worry because of a fear they will not be able to hold out—the fear of failure and of falling.

But the Shepherd of men is out ahead, and we can be assured of the protection of His strength. There is "the victory that overcometh the world, even our faith" (I John 5:4).

10. THOU ANOINTEST MY HEAD WITH OIL; MY CUP RUNNETH OVER

I WILL NEVER FORGET WHAT THE COACH SAID TO US THE first day I went out for football practice. He told us that football is a rough game and that if we expected to play it, we must also expect sometimes to get hurt.

So with life. If you expect to live it, you must also expect some bruises and hurt. That is just the way it is. And David, thinking of that fact, said in the Twenty-third Psalm, "Thou anointest my head with oil; my cup runneth over."

Sometimes, as the sheep grazed, its head would be cut by the sharp edge of a stone buried in the grass. There were briars to scratch and thorns to stick.

Then, some days the sheep had to walk steep paths under a hot, merciless sun. At the end of the day it would be tired and spent.

So the shepherd would stand at the door of the fold and examine each sheep as it came in. If there were hurt places the shepherd would apply soothing and healing oil. Instead of becoming infected, the hurt would soon heal.

Also, the shepherd had a large earthen jug of water, the kind of a jar which kept the water refreshingly cool through evaporation. As the sheep came in, the shepherd would dip down into the water with his big cup and bring it up brimful. The tired sheep drank deeply of the life-quickening draught.

Remember how, as little children, we would bruise a finger or stump a toe. We would come running to mama, who would kiss the hurt away. There was mystic healing in her loving concern.

As older children we still get hurt. A heart can be broken, a conscience can ache like an infected tooth, feelings can be hurt, the world can deal cruelly and harshly. One can become discouraged and tired. Sometimes the burden of life can be unbearable.

But also there is the tender Shepherd who understands the hurt of His children and is ever ready and able to minister to that hurt. Harry Lauder, the famous Scotch comedian, was grief-stricken at the loss of his son. But he found the Shepherd.

Later he was giving a concert in Chicago before an overflow crowd. He responded to repeated encores, and finally he quieted the audience and said very quietly, "Don't thank me. Thank the good God who put the songs in my heart."

Notice David said, "Thou anointest *my* head with oil, *my* cup . . ." He didn't say "our" heads. It is the singular, personal pronoun. All day long the shepherd has been concerned with the flock. But as they go into the fold he takes them one by one.

I had a professor in college one year who never did learn my name. Somehow, I never liked him very much. I read that Jesus said, "He calleth his own sheep by name" (John 10:3). I like that. It makes me feel important.

The Psalmist said, "He healeth the broken in heart. . . . He telleth the number of the stars" (Psalm 147:3,4). The power of the universe is power at *my* disposal.

11. SURELY GOODNESS AND MERCY SHALL FOLLOW ME ALL THE DAYS OF MY LIFE

IN THE PLAY "SOUTH PACIFIC," MARY MARTIN SANG A SONG that I think is wonderful. In that song she sang: "I'm stuck like a dope, with a thing called hope, I can't get it out of my heart."

David says the same thing in different words: "Surely goodness and mercy shall follow me all the days of my life." He is not wistfully thinking. He says *surely . . . surely . . . surely.*

David was an old man when he wrote the Twenty-third Psalm. He had seen tragedies and disappointments, but he also had come to know God—a God who knows the needs of His children and who abundantly provided for those needs, a God who can restore life and take away fear. In spite of dark clouds on the horizon, with a God like Him whom David knew, David was sure the sun would shine tomorrow.

We hear a lot about the wickedness of men and the destruction of the world. We know of bombs which can destroy cities with one awful blast. We tremble at the sound of dire predictions of the vengeful judgment of God.

But, somehow, as our minds are filled with the picture of the loving Shepherd leading his sheep we feel confident that He will lead us through the dark valleys.

One of the greatest teachers America has ever produced was Professor Endicott Peabody, headmaster of Groton for many years. One day at chapel he told his boys, "Remember, things in life will not always run smoothly. . . . The great fact to remember is that the trend of civilization is forever upward."

Those words stuck in the mind of one of his students, and about forty years later that student gave new heart to the nation when he said, "The only thing we have to fear is fear itself." Franklin D. Roosevelt will always be remembered for the hope he gave to a hopeless nation.

Many people think themselves into disaster. They feel a little bad and they fill their minds with the thought of being sick. They start out the day with dread of something bad happening. They look to tomorrow with fear and trembling.

There is a very successful teacher I have read about

who teaches people to sit quietly and conceive of their minds as being absolutely blank. Think of the mind as being a motion-picture screen.

Then flash on the screen of the mind a picture of something good you want to happen. Then take the picture off. Flash it on again. Take it off. Repeat that process until the picture becomes clear and sharp.

Through that process the picture becomes firmly established in one's conscious and subconscious minds. Then the professor tells the student to go to work to make that picture a reality, to maintain a spirit of prayer and faith.

It is amazing how completely and how quickly that picture in the mind will be developed in life.

Quit predicting disaster for your world and yourself. Say with the Psalmist, "This is the day which the Lord hath made; we will rejoice and be glad in it" (Psalm 118:24).

Begin the morning with hope. Plant this firmly in your mind, "Surely goodness and mercy shall follow me," and they will.

12. AND I WILL DWELL IN THE HOUSE OF THE LORD FOR EVER

It is always a thrilling experience to me to be downtown in Atlanta about 5 o'clock in the afternoon. The streets are filled with people and cars. Extra buses are running, and every one is packed with people standing. It is thrilling because the people are going home.

John Howard Payne had been away from home for nine years. One afternoon he stood at the window watching the throngs of people, happy, hurrying, going home. Suddenly he felt lonely, there in a Paris boardinghouse room.

Impatiently he turned from the window. He had work to do. It was perhaps an important play he was writing. He had no time for sentimental dreaming. But the mood and the memories of a little town on Long Island would not leave him.

He picked up a pencil and began writing:

'Mid pleasures and palaces though we may roam,
Be it ever so humble, there's no place like home.

And now for more than a hundred years that song has had a special place in the hearts of the people. There really is "no place like home."

But I also feel sadness as I watch the crowds going home. I know some who have no home to which to go. Some wander around seeking a cheap bed for the night, others can afford the nicest hotel suite in the city—still it isn't home.

I have dealt with a lot of alcoholics. Especially have a number of women told me how they started. They would go to an empty cheerless room or small apartment, be alone. There is not much fun in living alone. So many started drinking that way.

Much much more pathetic than seeing a homeless person at the end of the day is to find a person who is not sure of God and has no hope of the eternal home, who, at the close of life's day, can look forward only to some dark grave and oblivion.

David closes the Twenty-third Psalm with a mighty crescendo of faith when he declares, "I will dwell in the house of the Lord for ever."

One of the heart-stirring passages in Bunyan's *Pilgrim's Progress* is that in which "Mr. Feeble Mind" speaks of his hope of home. He says:

But this I am resolved on: to run when I can, to go when I cannot run, and to creep when I cannot go. . . . My mind is beyond the river that hath no bridge, though I am, as you see, but of a feeble mind.

Sometimes the greatest inspiration for living comes when your "mind is beyond that river that hath no bridge." Were it not for that assurance, many experiences of life would be unbearable.

David did not have the insights that we have. He never heard the words: "I am the resurrection, and the life: he that believeth in me, though he were dead, yet shall he live: and whosoever liveth and believeth in me shall never die" (John 11:25,26).

Just knowing intimately a God like he describes in the Twenty-third Psalm gave David assurance that at the close of life's day he would go home.

13 "HE KNOWS THE SHEPHERD"

There is a story—I do not know its source—of an old man and a young man on the same platform before a vast audience of people.

A special program was being presented. As a part of the program each was to repeat from memory the words of the Twenty-third Psalm. The young man, trained in the best speech technique and drama, gave, in the language of the ancient silver-tongued orator, the words of the Psalm.

"The Lord is my shepherd . . ." When he had finished, the audience clapped their hands and cheered, asking him for an encore so that they might hear again his wonderful voice.

Then the old gentleman, leaning heavily on his cane, stepped to the front of the same platform, and in feeble, shaking voice, repeated the same words—"The Lord is my shepherd . . ."

But when he was seated no sound came from the listeners. Folks seemed to pray. In the silence the young man stood to make the following statement:

"Friends," he said, "I wish to make an explanation. You asked me to come back and repeat the Psalm, but you remained silent when my friend here was seated. The difference? I shall tell you. I know the Psalm, but he knows the Shepherd!"

Perhaps the figure of the shepherd and the flock may mean little to the modern city dweller. Yet, if ever a people of this earth resembled a flock of frightened sheep it is now. Governments are afraid of each other. People are afraid of their governments, of other people, and of themselves.

This Psalm of David has sung its way across the barriers of time, race, and language. For twenty-five centuries it has been treasured in the hearts of people. Today it is more beloved than ever before.

The reason it lives? Not just because it is great literature. Because it tells that above all the strife and fears, the hungers and weaknesses of mankind, there is a Shepherd.

A shepherd who knows his sheep one by one, who is abundantly able to provide, who guides and protects and at the close of the day opens the door to the sheepfold— the house not made with hands.

In the quietness of the South Pole Admiral Byrd suddenly realized he was "not alone." That assurance caused faith to well up within him, and even though he stood in "the coldest cold on the face of the earth," he felt a comforting warmth.

The Twenty-third Psalm gives men that same assurance. That is why it lives in the hearts of men, regardless of race or creed.

PART II

GOD'S RULES FOR LIVING

And God spake all these words, saying,

I am the Lord Thy God, which have brought thee out of the land of Egypt, out of the house of bondage.

Thou shalt have no other gods before me.

Thou shalt not make unto thee any graven image, or any likeness of any thing that is in heaven above, or that is in the earth beneath, or that is in the water under the earth:

Thou shalt not bow down thyself to them, nor serve them: for I the Lord thy God am a jealous God, visiting the iniquity of the fathers upon the children unto the third and fourth generation of them that hate me;

And shewing mercy unto thousands of them that love me, and keep my commandments.

Thou shalt not take the name of the Lord thy God in vain; for the Lord will not hold him guiltless that taketh his name in vain.

Remember the sabbath day, to keep it holy.

Six days shalt thou labour, and do all thy work:

But the seventh day is the sabbath of the Lord thy God: in it thou shalt not do any work, thou, nor thy son, nor thy daughter, thy manservant, nor thy maidservant, nor thy cattle, nor thy stranger that is within thy gates:

*For in six days the Lord made heaven and
earth, the sea, and all that in them is,
and rested the seventh day: wherefore the
Lord blessed the sabbath day, and hallowed it.*

*Honour thy father and thy mother: that thy
days may be long upon the land which the
Lord thy God giveth thee.*

Thou shalt not kill.

Thou shalt not commit adultery.

Thou shalt not steal.

*Thou shalt not bear false witness against
thy neighbour.*

*Thou shalt not covet thy neighbour's house,
thou shalt not covet thy neighbour's wife,
nor his manservant, nor his maidservant, nor
his ox, nor his ass, nor any thing that is
thy neighbour's.* Exodus 20: 1-17

1. THOU SHALT HAVE NO OTHER GODS
BEFORE ME

SHORTLY AFTER MOSES LED THE CHILDREN OF ISRAEL AWAY
from the bondage of Egypt on their journey to the promised land, God called Moses up on Mt. Sinai. He must
have said something like this: "Moses, your people are
now headed toward prosperity. The land I have promised
to them is rich and productive and will supply not only
their needs, but much more. In fact, the land flows with
milk and honey. But, Moses, people cannot be made happy
and successful merely by the possession of things. The way
they live is more important than what they have. So, I am
going to give you ten rules for living. I want you to teach
the people these rules. If they live by them, I promise
they will be blessed. But I warn you, if they break these
rules they will be severely penalized. And one other thing,
Moses, these are to be the rules of living for all peoples of
all times. They will never go out of date, they will never
be repealed or changed."

We have those rules, known as The Ten Commandments, recorded in Exodus 20. They are not only the basis
of conduct, both moral and spiritual, but also the basis of
peace and prosperity for the individual and for the world.
The Bible says, "The fool hath said in his heart, There
is no God" (Psalm 14:1), and it is only a fool who thinks

45

he is big enough or smart enough to violate the unchangeable laws of the eternal God and get by with it. No man can break God's law, he breaks only himself.

Very important is the order in which God stated His laws. The first four deal with man's relationship with God, the last six with man's relationship with man. Before man can live rightly with each other, he must first get right with God. Someone has said, "The golden rule is my religion," but the golden rule is nobody's religion, because it is not a religion. It is merely the expression of religion.

As H. G. Wells put it, "Until a man has found God he begins at no beginning; he works to no end."

The first commandment is somewhat surprising. We would think that it would be, "Thou shalt believe in a God," a law against atheism. There is no such law. God took care of that in our creation. We do not teach a baby to hunger or to thirst, nature does that. However, we must train our children to satisfy their hungers and thirsts with the right things.

Man instinctively believes and worships. Nowhere does the Bible attempt to prove the existence of God. Man is created incomplete, and he cannot be at rest until there is a satisfaction of his deepest hunger, the yearning of his soul. The danger lies in that fact that man can pervert his worship instinct and make for himself a false god.

St. Augustine said, "My soul is restless until it finds it can rest in Thee, O God." No false god satisfies the longing of the soul, but we can, and many do, squander their lives seeking satisfaction from false objects of worship. So the first of God's rules for life is: "Thou shalt have no other gods before me."

At Vicksburg, Miss., an engineer showed me an almost dry channel. He explained that once the great Mississippi

46

river flowed there but now it had been changed into another channel, which had been dug. The flow of the river could not be stopped, but it could be diverted. So with our worship of God. Man is incomplete without an object of worship; the yearning of his soul demands attention. But man can turn from the one true God and make for himself another god. There have been people who worshiped the sun, or a star, or a mountain. In some countries people worship a cow, or a river, or something else. We think of those people as being primitive. They are, but no more primitive than multitudes of people in this enlightened land we call America. God said, "Thou shalt have no other gods before me," and that law of life we are guilty of breaking.

There are five objects of worship which multitudes today have put before God: wealth, fame, pleasure, power, and knowledge. While most of us have no idea of ever being really rich, we never become satisfied with what we can reasonably possess. Maybe that is good, except when that dissatisfaction obscures our feelings for God and diverts us in our search for God. I can become so interested in what I have that I forget the needs of my soul.

Most of us never expect to be famous, yet the little child says, "See how high I can jump or watch me run." We are born with the desire to be noticed. That is not wrong. God made us separate identities, and we do want to be known. Yet, as a minister, I counsel with many people who have wrecked their lives and destroyed their happiness simply because they have not received the attention they desired. Many get their feelings hurt at the smallest slight. We spend in America more money on cosmetics, for example, than we spend on the entire program of the kingdom of God. It isn't wrong to want to look our best.

47

But it is wrong when putting ourselves forward becomes our first desire, thus our god.

All men want to be happy but we make a mistake when we think pleasure is the way to get happiness. There is forgetfulness of life's routines in pleasures, but they do not satisfy the soul. Pleasure is like dope; gradually we must increase the dose with more excitement, more thrill, more sensation, until, eventually, we find ourselves groping among the tombstones of our dead passions. It is like making our meals out of pickles and pepper. One of our greatest temptations is to put pleasure before God.

Power is not wrong, neither is knowledge. The electric power in America is the equal of one hundred and fifty slaves for each of us and is a great blessing to us. But power worshiped turns us into little Hitlers. Knowledge is good, but the worship of knowledge destroys obedience, just as the worship of power destroys character.

To worship God leads us to be like God and to obey His will. Thus we become good and walk in the paths of right living when we have no other gods before God.

2. THOU SHALT NOT MAKE UNTO THEE ANY GRAVEN IMAGE

THE SECOND RULE OF GOD IS, "THOU SHALT NOT MAKE unto thee any graven image." This is the one rule that most people feel less guilty of breaking, yet more is said about this one in the Bible than any other. Primitive man found it hard to realize a God he could not see, so he made aids to assist his imagination, to bring reality into his worship. That is not wrong. Frank Boreham tells of a man who prayed with a vacant chair before him. He imagined God sitting in that chair, and it made his prayers more real.

On my desk are several copies of the Bible. I use them in my studying and devotional reading, yet they would be of value to me, even if I never opened them. Their very presence serves to remind me of God. Of course, one can worship anywhere, but worship is easier in the church building. Not only the building, but the ritual, the music and the sermon also are aids to worship.

The danger lies in the fact that it is so easy to worship the means instead of the goal. The Bible, churches, music, and ministers, and all our symbols and aids to worship are sacred only because they lead us to God. For example, denominationalism can be a violation of this rule. I am a Methodist, but I could be just as good a Christian as a Baptist or as a Presbyterian or in any denomination which says with Peter, "Thou art Christ, the son of the living God" (Matthew 16:16).

Even more dangerous than our aids to worship are some other images we make. We are told that "God created man in his own image" (Genesis 1:27). But to live a life in conformity with our creation is difficult. In fact, it is so difficult that all of us fall far short. Thus, instead of being like God, we seek to create Him in our own image. It is so much easier to make God like ourselves than for us to be like Him.

God tells us not to do wrong, but there are some

49

things we want to do, right or wrong. So we create a God who doesn't care what we do. We think of the God of the blue skies, majestic mountains and lovely flowers, but turn our backs on the God who said, "Ye have robbed me in tithes and offerings" (Malachi 3:8), or the God who said, "Whatsoever a man soweth, that shall he also reap" (Galatians 6:7). It has been well pointed out that Christ was not crucified because He said, "Consider the lilies, how they grow," but rather because He said, "Consider the thieves, how they steal."

It is so much easier to whittle God down to our size instead of repenting, changing our way of living, and being Godly ourselves. When Horace Bushnell was a college student he felt he was an atheist. One day a voice seemed to say to him, "If you do not believe in God, what do you believe?" He answered back, "I believe there is a difference between right and wrong." "Are you living up to the highest you believe?" the voice seemed to ask. "No," he said, "but I will." That day he dedicated his life to his highest belief. Years later, after he had been pastor of one church forty-seven years, he said, "Better than I know any person in my church, I know Jesus Christ." When he began conforming his life to his beliefs, instead of making his beliefs fit his life, he was led to a realization of God.

The very process of thinking requires mental pictures or images. Think of an apple and you see one in your imagination. Think of Abraham Lincoln and his face is flashed on the screen of your mind. And when one thinks of God he sees some picture of God. The danger lies in the fact that it can be the wrong picture, which can be tragic. One becomes like his image of God, and if it is the wrong image the man becomes wrong. So the Bible contains more warning in regard to God's second rule for life, "Thou shalt not make unto thee any graven image (Exodus 20:4), than in regard to any of the other ten.

Man sees a little of God in many forms, majesty in His mountains, greatness in His seas, loveliness in His flowers, righteousness in His saints. But all of these are insufficient. With Philip, the heart of each of us says, "Lord, show us the Father." Jesus replied, "He that hath seen me hath seen the Father" (John 14:8,9). The only perfect image of God we have is Christ, and that is sufficient.

As you see Him through the words of the Gospels—Matthew, Mark, Luke, and John, you are impressed with His eyes. Those who were with Him in the flesh neglected to tell us much about His physical appearance, but they could not forget His eyes. "And the Lord turned, and looked upon Peter" (Luke 22:61), and Peter broke down. Sometimes Jesus' eyes flashed with merriment, sometimes they melted in tenderness, and other times they were filled with stern rebuke. When I read, "The ways of man are before the eyes of the Lord" (Proverbs 5:21), I stop still in my tracks and think on my ways.

When we look at Jesus' face we know it was a happy face. Little children ran to get in His lap and clasp Him around His neck. People invited Him to their parties. Seeing God in Christ, we are not afraid of Him; instead we want to be closer to Him. We listen as He says, "Neither do I condemn thee; go and sin no more" (John 8:11), and we are ashamed of our sins, we want forgiveness, and we come to Him repenting and asking for His cleansing.

We look as "he steadfastly set his face to go to Jerusalem" (Luke 9:51). Though it meant death, He would not go back on the high purposes of His life. Seeing Him puts the steel in our own backbones to make the right decision. We watch as He walked seven miles to Emmaus to give hope to the downhearted (Luke 24:13-32), or as He gave a new chance to His friends who failed Him (John 20:19-31), and we take new heart and new hope.

How wonderful it is to see God. To encourage the early Christians who were bearing almost the unbearable John says to them that those who are faithful "shall see his face" (Rev. 22:4). The promise of seeing Him compensated for any sacrifice.

One thing more. After Thorwaldsen had completed his famous statue of Christ, he brought a friend to see it. Christ's arms were outstretched, His head bowed between them. The friend said, "But I cannot see His face." The sculptor replied, "If you would see the face of Christ you must get on your knees." He is the perfect image of God; let us have no other.

3. THOU SHALT NOT TAKE THE NAME OF THE LORD THY GOD IN VAIN

GOD'S THIRD RULE FOR LIVING IS, "THOU SHALT NOT TAKE the name of the Lord thy God in vain" (Exodus 20:7). The first rule is, put God first; the second is, get the right picture of God; the third is, think about God in the right way. What a person thinks about determines what he is. Hawthorne tells about the boy Ernest who would look longingly at the great stone face on the side of the mountain. It was a strong, kind, honorable face that thrilled the heart of this boy. There was a legend that some day a man would appear who would look like the Great Stone Face. Through all his childhood, and even after he became a man, Ernest kept looking at the great face and for the man who was like it. One day, when the people were discussing the legend, someone suddenly cried out, "Behold, behold, Ernest is himself the likeness of the Great Stone Face." Indeed he was; he had become like his thoughts.

The secret desires of our hearts eventually show up in our very appearance. Once someone wanted Lincoln to meet a certain man. "I do not want to see him," Lincoln said. But his friend protested, "You do not even know him." Lincoln replied, "I do not like his face." "A man cannot be held responsible for his face," the friend said. "Any grown man is responsible for the look on his face," the president insisted. And Lincoln was right. His own face was an example. Though homely and rough, in Lincoln's face one sees the very principles of sympathy and honesty which made him the greatest of all Americans.

Some psychologists have made extensive studies which show that a person's thoughts show up in his features. I have noticed that married couples who have lived together happily and harmoniously over a number of years come to look more like brother and sister than like husband and wife. As they live together, enjoy common experiences, think alike, they tend to look alike.

Ralph Waldo Emerson, one of the wisest of Americans, said, "A man is what he thinks about all day long." But that was not original with him. Marcus Aurelius, the wisest man of ancient Rome, said, "Our life is what our thoughts make of it." But before Aurelius said it, the wise men of the Bible said, "For as he thinketh in his heart, so is he" (Proverbs 23:7).

Once a football coach was worried because one of his boys who was capable of being a really great player was not showing up well. The coach decided to go to the boy's room one night and have a talk with him. There on the walls he saw a number of lewd and immoral pictures and then he understood. No boy could fill his mind with filth and trash and give his best performance on the field of play.

God's third rule is that we put something high and holy in our thinking to reverence, to be inspired by. St. Paul tells us: "Whatsoever things are true . . . honest . . . just . . . pure . . . lovely . . . of good report . . . think on these things" (Philippians 4:8). Those are qualities of God. As we think of Him it lifts and inspires our lives and makes us Godly.

There are at least three ways we profane God's name. First, by our language. We have all kinds of maniacs but one of the most common types we have in America is "swearomaniacs." It is alarming how our language is being filled with profanity. Many of our modern novels I would enjoy reading, but they contain such vile language that I will not read them because I do not want those words in my mind. The word "hell" has become one of our most common words. We say, "It is cold as hell," "It is hot as hell," "It is raining like hell," etc., etc. One man came in to see me recently who I thought used the word correctly. He said, "Preacher, I am in a helluva shape," and he was. Hell is down, not up, and to fill my mind with hell and the language of hell degrades my very soul. The word "profane" comes from two Latin words—"pro" meaning in front of and "fane" meaning temple. A profane word is one you would not use in church, and that is a mighty good way to judge the language we use.

Second, we take God's name in vain by not taking Him seriously. We admit there is a God, but our belief is merely lip service. Jesus said, "Whosoever heareth these sayings of mine, *and doeth them* . . ." (Matthew 7:24). To talk about God and not to live like God is profanity worse than vile language. Belief that does not make a radical difference in life is mere sham and hypocrisy. As Elton Trueblood put it, "An empty, meaningless faith may be worse than none."

A third way we take God's name in vain is by refusing His fellowship and His help. If I say a man is my friend, yet never want to be with him and do not call on him when I need his help, then I am lying when I use the word "friend." If I believe in a mechanic, then I will go to him when my car needs attention. If I believe in a physician I will call him when I become sick. Yet, when Adam and Eve sinned, they ran and hid from God. Their descendants have been doing likewise ever since.

On our lives is the stain of sin. There is only one who can forgive sin, and to refuse to pray, to close our Bibles, to turn our backs on the altar of His church is profanity of the worst sort. Once, when I was a little boy, I saw a soft drink truck which seemed unattended. I slipped one of the bottles in a pocket, and when I got around the bend of the road opened it. The driver stepped up just then and demanded payment, but I had no nickel. He sternly said, "Get the money for me in thirty minutes or I will put you in jail."

I ran home to my father and told him what I had done.

He neither condemned nor humiliated me. My own wrong had done that. Instead, he gave me a nickel and quietly said, "Go, pay the man." That is a picture of God. We do wrong and our very conscience condemns us to a hell from which we cannot escape. Then we remember, "If we confess our sins, he is faithful and just to forgive us our sins, and to cleanse us from all unrighteousness" (I John 1:9). Humbly we bow before Him and receive His forgiveness. Then we live for Him and according to His ways. That is belief that is not in vain.

4. REMEMBER THE SABBATH DAY, TO KEEP IT HOLY

EACH ONE OF GOD'S TEN RULES FOR LIVING IS VITAL, BUT in giving them to Moses, God said more about the fourth than any other. God needed only four words in regard to killing, but He used ninety-four words to tell us to "remember the sabbath day, to keep it holy." In the first place, God tells us to remember. In a scientific sense, one never forgets anything. Every thought we have is registered forever on our minds, but, practically, we can forget almost everything. We forget dates and names, we forget duties and even God. Some things we forget on purpose because the remembrance of them is not pleasant. Other things we forget because our minds are preoccupied with other matters. We forget to keep God's day. But God says man needs to set aside a day each week to keep it holy, and to fail to keep that day holy is to suffer.

In the first place, God gave to man the Sabbath as a reward for his labor. The man who labors deserves to rest, and to forget God's gift is only to cheat ourselves.

In his book, *East River*, Sholem Asch quotes the words of an old Jew, Moshe Wolf, in regard to the Lord's day. It is about the best statement on keeping the Sabbath I know. He said: "When a man labors not for a livelihood, but to accumulate wealth, then he is a slave. Therefore it is that God granted the Sabbath. For it is by the Sabbath that we know that we are not working animals, born to eat and to labor. We are men. It is the Sabbath which is man's goal; not labor, but the rest which he earns from his labor. It was because the Jews made the Sabbath holy to God that they were redeemed from slavery in Egypt. It was by the Sabbath that they proclaimed that they were not slaves, but free men."

Second, God gave us Sunday because every man needs to be re-created. Just as a battery can run down and need to be recharged, so can a person. Gerald Kennedy tells of two parties who started out across the plains in the pioneer days, going west to California. One was led by a religious man and one was led by an irreligious man. One group stopped all of each Lord's day for worship and rest. The other party was so anxious to reach the gold of California that it would not take time to stop. The men drove every day. The amazing thing is that the party which observed the Sabbath arrived first. We have now well established the fact in our own nation that one can do more work in six days, even in five, than in seven. A run-down person is an unproductive person.

Also, we need to re-create our souls. A group of American explorers went to Africa. They employed some native guides. The first day they rushed, as they did also on the second, third, and every day. On the seventh day they noticed the guides sitting under a tree. "Come on," they shouted. One of the guides replied, "We no go today. We rest today to let our souls catch up with our bodies." For that purpose, God says, "Remember the Sabbath."

We have spent so much time arguing about what we should not do on Sunday that we sometimes forget what we should do. God gave us the day, not as a time of prohibitions but rather to give us opportunity for the finest and most important things of life. An old miner once explained to a visitor, "I let my mules spend one day a week outside the mines to keep them from going blind." And the person who does not spend time away from the daily grind of life goes blind in his soul. The philosopher Santayana tells us, "A fanatic is one who, having lost sight of his aim, redoubles his effort." And much of the feverish haste we see today is by aimless, purposeless people. God says we need a day a week to keep our aim. Or, as Carlyle put it, "The man who does not habitually worship is but a pair of spectacles behind which there is no eye."

As a pastoral counselor, I have seen many people who had lost their nerve control. Life for many had become a miserable experience. But it is rare, very rare, to find an uncontrolled person who regularly worships God and keeps His day holy. We have a slang expression, "That got my goat." That phrase has an interesting beginning. Owners of sensitive, high-strung race horses used to keep a goat in the stalls with the horses. The very presence of the calm, relaxed goat helped the horses to relax. On the day before an important race rival owners would sometimes steal another owner's goats. Thus the horse would not run its best the next day.

Well, we get sensitive and high-strung, and thus we falter in the race of life. Man needs relaxed re-creation and spiritual inspiration. Oliver Wendell Holmes said: "I have in my heart a small, shy plant called reverence; I cultivate that on Sundays." And well it will be if we all cultivate the plant of reverence within our hearts, because, as Dostoevski reminds us, "A man who bows down to nothing can never bear the burden of himself." Many of our fears, worries, and nervous tensions would be saved if we kept this fourth rule of God.

We are in too big a hurry, and we run by far more than we catch up with. The Bible tells us to "be still, and know that I am God" (Psalm 46:10). Beauty doesn't shout. Loveliness is quiet. Our finest moods are not clamorous. The familiar appeals of the Divine are always in calm tones, a still, small voice. Here is the New Testament picture of Jesus: "Behold, I stand at the door, and knock: if any man hear my voice, and open the door, I will come in to him, and will sup with him, and he with me" (Revelation 3:20). The Divine is not obtrusive. He bursts in no one's life unbidden. He is reserved and courteous. "We need a day when we can hear such a voice as His. A day when we give the Highest a hearing," as Dr. Fosdick so well said.

Just as men build telescopes to gain a clearer view of the stars, so almost since the dawn of civilization, have men built churches and set aside a day to worship, in order to gain a clearer view of God and the high purposes of life. "Remember the sabbath day, to keep it holy," said God.

5. HONOR THY FATHER AND THY MOTHER

GOD GAVE US TEN RULES TO LIVE BY. THE FIRST FOUR DEAL with our relationship to Him. The last five deal with our relationship with other people. The fifth rule has been called the centerpiece of God's law. "Honor thy father and thy mother" involves both our relationship with God and with our fellow men. When God made man He also set up the pattern by which men must live together. First, a man and a woman come together in marriage, and out of the union come children. The parents provide love, care, and control for the child, and, in reality, the parent is to the child its first god. As the child learns to love and respect its parents, so later does it love and respect God.

Also, the parents are the greatest social influence on the life of the child. It is in the home that a child first learns to respect the personalities of others, to have regard for the rights of others, to learn obedience to the laws for the welfare of all people. A child's respect for both authority and democracy usually must begin, if it begins at all, in the home. So, upon the parent and child relationship in the home rests almost our entire civilization.

Of course, the relationship of the parent and child is an ever changing one. At first, the baby must be carried. Later, it learns to walk, holding its mother's hand; still later, it learns to walk alone. Up to about ten the child thinks its parents know everything. At about sixteen the child is not so sure about its parents. At nineteen the child feels it has surpassed the parents in knowledge and at twenty-two he completely outgrows the parent. But at thirty we remember that our parents were right about a lot of things, and at forty we decide they were just about perfect. That is usually about the normal process.

As I study this rule of God to honor our parents, to me it means three things: (1) It means that the parents must be honorable.

Once a mother carried her little boy to the zoo. He was asking about each of the animals, and when he saw some little ones in a cage, he asked, "What are those?" The mother told him they were little wildcats. He then asked, "Why are they wild cats?" We know the answer. Their mamas and papas were wildcats. Usually, children are the reflection of their parents, because it is the most natural thing for a child so to reverence its parents that it will live according to the principles it sees in them.

When Quentin Roosevelt was on the Western Front during World War I, an observer said, "I come here especially to tell you how millions of Americans appreciate the splendid way in which the sons of Theodore Roosevelt are acquitting themselves in this conflict." "Well, you see," Quentin replied, "it's up to us to practice what father preaches. I'm Roosevelt's son. It's up to me to live like a Roosevelt."

General Douglas MacArthur expressed the thought I have when he said: "By profession I am a soldier and take pride in that fact. But I am prouder to be a father. My hope is that my son, when I am gone, will remember me not from battle, but in the home, repeating with him one simple prayer, 'Our Father which art in heaven.'"

That is the first meaning of this rule for living which God gave us.

(2) To "honor thy father and thy mother" means not only that parents should be honorable, it means also that children should recognize, respect, and love their parents. It seems to me that just common decency would cause us to honor our parents. Once, when I was pastor of a little country church, I was out visiting and saw a woman picking cotton. I stopped and went down in the field to speak to her. She told me her son had been offered a job in the near-by furniture factory, which would pay good wages, and that she had said to him, "Son, since your father died, I have been working this field to support you in school. You lack just one more year now, and I can keep on so you can finish."

Her hands were rough and calloused, her face was weather-beaten and her back was stooped, but as that boy looks at her, if he does not feel she is the most beautiful woman in all the world, then he is utterly unworthy of her. Maybe our parents made some mistakes, but they gave us life, they nurtured us as babies, and they loved us, which is more, far more, than any one else has done or ever can do.

(3) But this rule of life includes more than our immediate parents. It means that we must recognize our debt to the past and be thankful for it. As I stand in my pulpit each Sunday I am proud to be there. But as I look at the congregation I see men and women who have been there for forty, fifty, and even sixty years. For nearly a hundred years consecrated people have worked to build the church in which I preach. Back of that is upwards of two thousand years of Christian history, "in spite of dungeon, fire and

sword." And still beyond are the prophets of old of Abraham's faith. All the chance and opportunity I have come from the contributions of others better than I. So nothing I could ever do would be equal to what has been done for me.

So many things came crowding in on me the night my father died. I thought of the struggle of his youth to get what little education he could and the even greater struggle to give his children a better chance than he had. I thought of how as a little boy I went with him to his country churches and how proud of him I was as he preached. Of how that after I became a preacher I would preach for him and he for me. And now his voice was still. My first feeling of loneliness was overcome by the realization that now I had not only my work to do, but also his to carry on. Sometimes people tell me I attempt to do too much, but I am caught up by the conviction that I must do the work of two men.

So it is with all of us. What we have and what we are is because of what we have received. We must not only be vessels in which our heritage is carried to the next generations, we must increase that wealth. Each of us is an investment. Our responsibilities differ in that to some have been given five talents, to others two, and to others one. But to take what we have received, be it little or much, and to fail to increase it, is to become a "wicked and slothful servant."

Faith of our fathers, we will love
Both friend and foe in all our strife;
And preach thee, too, as love knows how,
By kindly words and virtuous life:

63

Faith of our fathers, holy faith,
We will be true to thee till death.

—FREDERICK W. FABER

6. THOU SHALT NOT KILL

GOD MADE US TO LIVE WITH EACH OTHER, AND THE VERY process of living requires certain rules. Without rules to go by the process of living together would be impossible. Here is a highway over which many cars can travel safely if they obey such rules as driving on the right side, not passing except with proper clearance, maintaining a reasonable speed, etc. To break the rules makes the highway unsafe for all who use it, and, instead of an instrument of service, the highway becomes an instrument of death and destruction. Now, life can be good or bad—it depends on how well we keep the rules as we go along. God laid down five rules to govern our relationships with each other. The first one is: "Thou shalt not kill" (Exodus 20:13).

First, this applies to our own selves. We did not create our lives, and we do not have the authority to destroy our lives. The very fact of life carries with it an inescapable obligation to live. Frequently the question of suicide comes up. Clearly, it is a violation of God's law. Now as to what God does about one who so breaks His law I gladly leave to Him. and I do not know what the eternal result is. God reserves the judgment for Himself, and surely He takes into account all the circumstances and one's mental responsibility.

Not only suicide, murder, too, is prohibited. All sensible and sane people agree we should not take a gun and shoot either ourselves or another person. But involved in this rule are the laws of health, which to violate is to kill, even though it may be by degrees. This commandment forbids exposing ourselves or others to needless physical risks, such as excessive speed on the highways, unsafe working conditions, improper housing, harmful pleasures, and the like.

Also forbidden is exposing ourselves or others to needless moral or spiritual risks. We can kill by killing faith or ideals. In talking about a man who had leaped from the window of a high building, an old negro janitor who knew the man's life very wisely said, "When a man has lost God, there ain't nothing to do but jump." Jotham was a king who did not go to church. Being a strong man, he still remained morally upright. But others, seeing his example, did not go either. The result was, "And the people did yet corruptly" (II Chronicles 27:2). Also, such things as ingratitude, neglect, cruelty, indifference can be slow but sure instruments of death.

Also forbidden are the destructive emotions of men: fear, hate, jealousy, anger, envy, anxiety, excessive grief, and the others. To counteract them requires developing within our lives the healing and life-giving emotions, such as, faith, hope, laughter, creativeness, and love. Love, for example, is a process of giving; giving through love destroys selfishness which in turn, results in the destruction of wrong desire, which, in turn, results in the destruction of jealousy, which, in turn, results in the end of hate which, in turn, will eliminate the hate murders.

It is a very involved process, not nearly as simple as I state it here. But take excessive grief, for another example. That is a form of self-pity, which grows out of selfishness, which is the lack of outgoing love. "Thou shalt not kill" involves the entire realm of living and the reasons for life. To reverence the life of all men is God's law for us.

To live and let live is only half the meaning of "Thou shalt not kill." Positively, it means to live and help live. Jesus did not find it necessary to warn us against becoming gangsters and murderers, but very clearly does He condemn those who pass by on the other side of a wounded brother. The very foundation of this commandment is the fact that God values every man as He values me. One God who hath made of one blood all nations. One God who is the Father and all men who are brothers. The rule of living means that we look at all men in the proper light.

Lorado Taft, in setting up a statue of a boy by Donatello, put some lights around it. First, he had them down on the floor shining up on the boy's face. As he stepped back and looked at it he was shocked—the boy looked like a moron. He changed the lights. He tried every arrangement. Finally, he put them up above, until they came down on the boy's face. Then he stood back and smiled, for the boy looked like an angel.

That is a wonderful story. When you look at men from merely the earthly level some do look like morons. Others look inferior, and it is so easy to feel, "Those people do not matter." But when we look at man, any man, through the eyes of the Christian faith, with the light streaming down on him from God, then you see the divinity

66

in him. All life becomes sacred, and you say, "I must not kill—I must help to live."

One of the high moments of *Quo Vadis* was in the arena at night. Queen Lygia had been captured in the early days of Christianity and brought to Rome. Also, her servant Ursus, a giant. Both were Christians and were to be fed to the lions. Their hour came, thousands were in the arena, and the giant Ursus was led to the center. He kneels in prayer and intends to stay on his knees, offering no resistance. Then dashes in a wild bull, with Lygia the object of his fury.

Seeing the danger of his queen, Ursus seizes the horns of the bull. It was a tremendous struggle, brute strength is pitted against the strength and heart of the giant. Slowly the feet of each sinks into the sand and then slowly the head of the bull begins to go down. In the quietness the people hear the cracking of the bones in the bull's neck as Ursus breaks it. Gently Ursus frees his queen and carries her to safety.

That is the positive side of living. Such beasts as hate, greed, prejudice, war, ignorance, poverty, disease, leave us unmoved until they endanger someone we love. It is then we exert all our strength against them. And as we come to love all men, so we enter the war against all enemies of men.

One thing more. I know a man who, though well past seventy years, is spending the major portion of his energy in helping to build a school. He told me that he would never be able to see many of the children who would be blessed by his school, but he knew they would be coming and he wanted to prepare for them. That same man is concerned about the conservation of natural resources, about every matter which will make life fuller for the next generation. So much concerned that he gives himself for—

The day in whose clear-shining light,
All wrong shall stand revealed,
When justice shall be clothed with might,
And every hurt be healed.

—FREDERICK L. HOSMER

7. THOU SHALT NOT COMMIT ADULTERY

FOR A MINISTER TO SPEAK ON THE SEVENTH COMMANDMENT —"Thou shalt not commit adultery"—requires unusual tact and reverence, lest even his rebukes should be like the lights of the Pharos, which sometimes helped to wreck the vessels they were meant to save. It is a sin which should be discussed as little as possible, but, since God lists it in seriousness next to murder, and since a large area of our modern society tends to consider it more a harmless moral breach than a breaking of God's eternal law, we need to be reminded that God says, "Thou shalt not . . ."

Morris Wee tells that one day his theological professor said to the class, "About fifty per cent of all human misery is caused by the violation of this commandment." That seems an extreme statement—"About fifty per cent . . ." The students did not believe it, but after a score of years in the ministry, Dr. Wee says he now knows it is so.

Sit with me in my study in a church on a main thoroughfare of a great city. Listen to my telephone, read my mail, talk with many who come in person. You, too, will begin to believe the professor was right.

Let me ask three questions which I shall try to answer: What is adultery? Why is it wrong? What can one who has violated the law do about it?

Adultery is violation of the marriage vow of faithfulness to each other. Any sex experience outside the marriage bond is adultery. Jesus goes even further and says lust in our hearts, even though unexpressed, is adultery (Matthew 5:27, 28). We know that sometimes wrong thoughts slip into the mind and we cannot help it, but to turn that thought into lust means to keep it in the mind, secretly to enjoy it, to make friends with it.

It is wrong because God said it is wrong. He said it is wrong because it hurts people. Any person who has any conscience at all feels a deep sense of guilt over the violation of this law. People have told me of stealing and justifying it to the point where they feel they have done no wrong. A man can even commit murder under certain circumstances and not feel he has done wrong. But I have never had one person to name the sin of adultery and seek to justify it. We know it is wrong, and there is no circumstance under which it can be justified. Thus, having broken the law, our mind becomes wounded. David's reaction to the transgression of this law is universal: "My sin is ever before me" (Psalm 51:3).

It is wrong because it brings further wrong. A wound in the mind is like a wound in the body. Cut a finger and it won't hurt much, but if the cut becomes infected, the infection will get into the blood stream, course through the body and eventually kill one. Sorrow is a wound. It cuts deeply and hurts terribly, but it is a clean wound, and, unless bitterness, resentment or self-pity gets into the wound, it will heal. But when I do wrong the result is an unclean wound, which will not heal. It robs me of my peace of mind, it makes my conscience hurt, it distorts my thinking, it sets up conflicts within me, it weakens my will power, it destroys my soul.

Phillips Brooks said, "Keep clear of concealment, keep clear of the need of concealment. It is an awful hour when the first necessity of hiding anything comes. When there are eyes to be avoided and subjects which must not be touched, then the whole bloom of life is gone."

The main reason adultery is wrong is that it destroys marriage. You remember the lovely scene in the story, "Mrs. Miniver." They had just acquired a new car and she also had a new hat. When they go to bed that night they are not sleepy but are thinking of their good fortune. Mrs. Miniver says, "We are the luckiest people." Her husband asks, "Why, because of the new car or the new hat?" "No dear, it is because we have each other." For a happy marriage, a lot of things are not necessary. Money and the things that money can buy are good to have but can be done without. But in marriage there are two things which must exist. First, a solid affection, a love for each other entirely different from the love for anyone else. Second, complete trust in each other. Adultery destroys both.

Beautiful was the custom of the Cherokee Indians. In the marriage ceremony the couple would join hands across a running stream to signify that forever their lives would flow together.

Suppose one is guilty of adultery, can anything be done

about it? Turn to the eighth chapter of St. John's Gospel and read there how a guilty one was brought before Jesus. The crowd had no solution but to stone her. They asked Jesus' opinion. His solution to any wrong never was stoning. He hated the sin but He never ceased to love the sinner.

When I was a little boy living in Tate, Georgia, I once was deeply impressed with a story I heard Mr. Sam Tate tell. There was an habitual drunkard in the community, and one morning he said, "Sam, the boys rocked me last night." "Maybe they were trying to make a better man out of you," replied Mr. Tate. "Well," the poor fellow said, "I never heard of Jesus throwing rocks at a man to make him better."

In the midst of the crowd with the guilty woman before Him Jesus said nothing. Instead, He stooped down and began writing on the ground. I wonder what He wrote. After a while, He spoke softly, yet so all could hear, "He that is without sin among you, let him cast the first stone." Again He stooped down and wrote on the ground. Perhaps He knew that crowd of self-righteous people who were always ready to push somebody further down. My guess is He wrote such words as "liar," "thief," "hypocrite." One by one, the men who were so ready to condemn dropped their rocks and shame-facedly slipped away.

Now comes one of the grandest scenes in the entire Bible. The matchless Saviour is alone with the woman. Not one harsh word comes from His lips. Not even a look of rebuke. Instead, gently and tenderly He says, "Neither do I condemn thee: go, and sin no more." In my mind I see her as she stands. She rises to her full height, her chin goes up and her shoulders back as the burden of her soul is lifted. She is caught up in the power of new self-respect and another chance.

Tradition has it that it was she who stood by Mary, the virgin mother, at the foot of the cross that day. Also, that it was she who first received the message of His resurrection and was given the blessed privilege of telling others. To announce His birth, God sent His angels from heaven. That privilege was not given to mortal man. But to tell of His living again, this fallen one was selected. Whatever my sin, Christ, and Christ alone, can take away the guilt and let me live again.

8. THOU SHALT NOT STEAL

GOD'S EIGHTH RULE FOR LIFE, "THOU SHALT NOT STEAL," IS the foundation of our entire economic system, because it recognizes the fact that one has a right, a God-given right, to work, earn, save, and own. To take away from one that which is rightfully his is wrong in the sight of God. In the creation story we are told how God made the earth, the sea and everything on the earth and in the sea. Then He made man and gave to man dominion over His creation (Genesis 1:26). Actually no person owns anything. All belongs to God, but while man is on earth he has the God-given right of possession. To deny any man that right violates the very basis of God's creation.

Since the beginning of time various economic systems

have been tried, but only one will really work and that is free enterprise by Godly people. It has been pointed out that the first Christians tried a form of collective ownership, but it also needs to be remembered that their experiment failed and they soon abandoned it. St. Paul writes, "If any would not work, neither should he eat" (II Thessalonians 3:10).

Once Jesus told a story of a man who was taking a journey from Jerusalem down to Jericho. He fell among thieves, who robbed and beat him and left him wounded by the roadside. A priest and a Levite came along, saw the man, but passed by on the other side. A Samaritan came along, helped the man, and made financial provision for his keep while he could not care for himself (Luke 10:30, 37). In that simple story we have clearly demonstrated the three possible philosophies of wealth. The interpretation is not original with me.

First, the philosophy of the thieves is: "What belongs to my neighbor belongs to me and I will take it." There is aggressive stealing—by the robber, the embezzler, and all the others. Included also is such a thing as living beyond one's means. To go in debt without a reasonable probability of being able to pay back is stealing. To fail to give an honest day's work is also stealing. Once a servant girl applied for membership in a church, but could give no evidence of her conversion and was about to be sent away. The pastor asked, "Is there no evidence which would indicate a change of heart?" She replied, "Now I don't sweep under the rugs in the house where I am employed." "It is enough," he said, "we will receive her into our fellowship."

Also, we can steal from another his inner supports. One does not live by bread alone. When Mark Twain

73

married Olivia Langdon she was a very devout Christian. He was so unsympathetic with her faith that gradually she gave up her religious practices. Later, there came into her life a very deep sorrow. He urged, "Livy, lean on your faith." Sadly she told him, "I can't. I haven't any left." To his dying day he was haunted by the fact that he had taken from her that which had meant so much.

Shakespeare put his finger on the worst form of stealing when he told us: "He that filches from me my good name robs me of that which not enriches him and makes me poor indeed." Before repeating something bad about another person, ask yourself these three questions: Is it true? Is it necessary for me to tell it? Is it kind to tell it?

There are many ways of aggressive stealing.

Second, not only can we steal by taking from another, we also steal by withholding from our fellows. The philosophy of the priest and Levite in the story of the Good Samaritan was: "What belongs to me is mine and I will keep it." Some people's measure of success is how much they can grab hold of and hold on to. As I go about I see a lot of "coffin" men. They have room for themselves and nobody else. They live in the spirit of the little girl who said;

I gave a little party this afternoon at three;
'Twas very small, three guests in all, just I, myself and me.
Myself ate up all the sandwiches, while I drank up the tea,
And it was I who ate the pie, and passed the cake to me.

Jesus told us of such a man. He was very successful and accumulated more than he needed. What did he do? "I will pull down my barns, and build greater; and there will I bestow all my fruits and my goods." Saving is a

74

virtue, but a very dangerous virtue. Every dollar I possess carries with it a corresponding obligation. This man was so blinded by his greed that he failed to see his opportunities and his obligations. The result was he lost his soul" (Luke 12:16-21).

The prophet Malachi asked the sobering question, "Will a man rob God?" He answers by saying we have robbed God "in tithes and offerings" (Malachi 3:8). It is a clear law of God that we return unto Him ten per cent of all He permits us to possess, and it is a fearful thing to come before Him in judgment with His money that we had kept or used for ourselves.

Third, the Good Samaritan saw his brother's need and his philosophy was, what belongs to me belongs to others, and I will share it. Let us never forget that the right of private enterprise and ownership is not something we have earned. Rather is it our God-given privilege. God expresses His faith in us, but He also demands an accounting. Ability, talents, opportunity, material resources are really not ours. They are God's investments in us. And like any wise investor, God expects dividends. Suppose I put my money into a company and the officers of the company use all the profits for themselves. I would be cheated. Likewise can we cheat God.

But how can I give to God what is rightfully His? There is only one way; that is in service to others. So, the positive meaning of "Thou shalt not steal" is consecrated service, both of my material resources and of my life. Bernard Shaw once said, "A gentleman is one who puts more into life than he takes out."

One thing more. Once Jesus went home with a man named Zacchaeus. Later on, we hear Zacchaeus saying,

"Lord, the half of my goods I give to the poor; and if I have taken any thing from any man I restore him four-fold." Jesus replied, "This day is salvation come to this house" (Luke 19:1,9). Stealing demands restitution. No man has room for both Christ and dishonest gains. He must decide between the two. It is often not an easy decision to make. But it may help to decide by asking ourselves, "For what shall it profit a man, if he shall gain the whole world, and lose his own soul?" (Mark 8:36.)

9. THOU SHALT NOT BEAR FALSE WITNESS AGAINST THY NEIGHBOR

OF THE TEN COMMANDMENTS, THE ONE WE BREAK THE most is the ninth—"Thou shalt not bear false witness against thy neighbor." One reason for this is that we talk most about people. Those of great minds discuss ideas, people of mediocre minds discuss events, and those of small minds discuss other people. Most of us have never made much mental development. Another reason we break this commandment is because it ministers to our own pride. It takes some of the sting out of our own failures if we can rub off the glitter of someone else's crown. It is a sure sign of an inferiority complex when a person tells of the faults of another. Back of much gossip is jealousy.

However, hardly anybody feels guilty of violating this law. I have had people confess to me the breaking of every one of the Ten Commandments except this one. I have never heard a person admit gossiping. We say, "I don't mean to talk about him, but . . ." and off we go. We assume a self-righteous attitude which we feel gives us license to condemn sin. But all the time we enjoy talking about the sin, and, in a back-handed way, brag of ourselves because we have not done exactly what the person we are telling about has done.

Sometimes our gossip takes the form of a false sympathy. "Isn't it too bad how Mr. Blank beats his wife? I am so sorry for her." Or maybe we just ask a question. "Is it true that Mr. and Mrs. Blank are on the verge of divorce?" That is the method of the devil. He would not accuse Job of any wrongdoing. Instead, he merely asked, "Doth Job fear God for nought?" (Job 1:9). The mere question raises a suspicion as to Job's sincerity.

Then we gossip just by listening. There cannot be a noise unless there is an ear to hear it. A noise is caused by the vibrations of the ear drums. And neither can there be a bit of gossip without an ear to hear. The law holds the receiver of stolen goods as guilty as the thief. It is really an insult to you for someone to tell you of the vices of another man, because in so doing he is passing judgment, not only on the subject of his gossip, but also on you. If someone tells you a dirty joke his very action is saying that he thinks of you as one interested in dirty jokes. For one to tell you of another's sins means that the gossiper's opinion of you is that you would be glad to know such things. It is really an insult to you.

Usually we do not mean to hurt others whom we talk about. We think of talebearing as a bit of harmless pastime. But let us remember the words of our Lord, "Judge not,

77

that ye be not judged. For with what judgment ye judge, ye shall be judged: and with what measure ye mete, it shall be measured to you again" (Matthew 7:1,2). That statement scares me. It drives me to my knees. I want God to be kinder toward me than I have been toward others. Don't you?

"So live," advised Will Rogers, "that you would not be ashamed to sell the family parrot to the town gossip." That is good advice, but I am afraid not many of us have lived up to it. Therefore, we should remind ourselves of the old saying:

> *There is so much good in the worst of us,*
> *And so much bad in the best of us,*
> *That it ill behooves the best of us,*
> *To talk about the rest of us.*

A modern translation of Jesus' words in Matthew 7:5 is: "Thou hypocrite, first cast out the two by four out of thine own eye; and then shalt thou see clearly to cast out the splinter out of thy brother's eye."

Whenever I think of the ninth commandment, "Thou shalt not bear false witness," I am haunted by a story which Pierre Van Paassen tells in his book, *The Days of Our Years*. I have seen the story quoted in many places, but would like to tell it briefly again. There was a hunchback by the name of Ugolin who fell sick. He never knew his father, and his mother was a drunken outcast. He had a lovely sister named Solange. Because she loved Ugolin so much and because she could get the money to buy his medicine in no other way, she sold her body on the streets.

People talked so harshly that Ugolin drowned himself in the river, and Solange shot herself. For their funeral the little village church was crowded. The minister mounted the pulpit and began his sermon:

"Christians" [*the word was like a whip-lash*], *"Christians, when the Lord of life and death shall ask me on the Day of Judgment, 'Where are thy sheep?' I shall not answer Him. When the Lord asks me the second time, 'Where are thy sheep?' I will yet not answer Him. But when the Lord shall ask me a third time, 'Where are thy sheep?' I shall hang my head in shame and I will answer Him, 'They were not sheep, Lord, they were a pack of wolves.'"*

In a recent sermon I said the person who talks about one who sins is worse than the one who actually commits the sin. That is a rather extreme statement which I made extemporaneously in an off-guarded moment. I am not sure it is true. Yet I am not sure it isn't true. What do you think? Before you answer turn over and read the story about Noah getting drunk (Genesis 9:20,27).

Noah was a preacher. Now, it is shameful for any person to get drunk, but for one who wears the royal purple of the prophet it is a double shame. Noah lay in his tent disgracefully naked. After a while his son Ham came and saw his father and he went out and told it. Noah's two other sons, Shem and Japheth, refused to look upon their father. Instead, they backed into the tent and covered their father with a garment.

Many generations later, when the author of Hebrews writes of the great men of faith, he tells of Noah's mighty work and does not remember his fall against him (Hebrews 11:7). Undoubtedly God forgot it also. Japheth and Shem were blessed of God and they prospered. But Ham, the son who told of his father's nakedness, was cursed and was condemned to the life of a servant. Maybe, after all, he who actually commits the sin comes out better than he who tells about it.

Jim was considered the bad boy of the community. He was blamed for everything. He took his whippings at school without complaint and with no tears. But one year a new schoolteacher came, and when something happened, naturally everyone blamed that boy. He expected the usual beating. Instead, the teacher said, "Now, let Jim tell his side." To the surprise of everyone, Jim began to cry. When the teacher asked, "What is the matter?" Jim replied, "This is the first time anybody ever said I had a side."

One of my favorite verses of Scripture is: "Brethren, if a man be overtaken in a fault, ye which are spiritual, restore such a one in the spirit of meekness; considering thyself, lest thou also be tempted" (Galatians 6:1).

10. THOU SHALT NOT COVET

GOD'S FINAL RULE FOR LIFE IS, "THOU SHALT NOT COVET." Of course, that does not mean that all desire is wrong. Without desires, no one would have any ambition, we would not work, we would not make progress. To covet means that I think of myself and of what I can get. God would have us forget ourselves and think of what we can give. This same commandment is stated by Jesus in a positive way. St. Paul quotes Him as saying, "It is more blessed to give than to receive" (Acts 20:35).

The word "covet" comes from a Greek word which means, "grasping for more." No matter how much one gets, he is always discontented, and, eventually, after covetousness drives him unmercifully through life, it kills him and leaves him with nothing. Tolstoy told a story which illustrates the activity of covetousness. A peasant was offered all the land he could walk around in a day. So the man started, hurrying to get around as much as possible. But the exertion he put forth was so great that he fell dead just as he got back to where he had begun. He ended up with nothing.

God gave these ten laws for our good. He wants us to be our very best and to get the most that is possible out of life. His last rule brings us to the very climax of living, which is contentment. That is what we all want. Contentment gives peace and joy in our minds and hearts, which is the reward of living God's way. But this must be the last of the ten rules. Without the other nine, it is impossible to observe. How does one root out of his life wrong desire? It is by filling his life with right desires.

The best summary of the Ten Commandments is the one Jesus gave: "Thou shalt love the Lord thy God with all thy heart, and with all thy soul, and with all thy mind. . . . Thou shalt love thy neighbor as thyself" (Matthew 22:37, 39). Put God and others first, get something into your mind greater than yourself. In so doing you lose yourself, selfishness is blotted out; instead of making ourselves miserable by what we do not have, we begin to gain the blessed thrill of giving what we can give.

There is a good story of four men who climbed a

mountain. The first complained that his feet hurt. The second had a greedy eye and kept wishing for each house and farm he could see. The third saw clouds and was worried for fear that it might rain. But the fourth fixed his eyes on the marvelous view. In looking away from himself and from the valley below, the little worries which made the others so unhappy were unnoticed.

And when in our view appears the vision of God and of opportunities of service to our fellow men, we experience, not misery-giving selfishness, but the fruits of the spirit. In losing our selfish desires, we gain love, joy, peace, long-suffering, gentleness, goodness, faith, meekness, and temperance. Those are the fruits of the spirit, the results of living God's way (Galatians 5:22,23).

As we study the Ten Commandments we become almost overwhelmed by a sense of guilt and of shame. We have not lived up to God's rules; in so many places have we failed.

I do not know what the final Judgment Day of God is like. We have a mental picture of Him sitting as the judge with a big book before Him in which are listed all our transgressions. Maybe it will not be that way at all. However, one thing we know, there will be a judgment. How will you plead? Did you worship idols in the place of God? —Guilty! Did you fail to live up to your highest belief, profane God's name, pay no respect to His day?—Guilty! Were you untrue to the best of the past, did you fail to support life as you might have done, were you dishonest and unclean?—Guilty! Did you bear false witness, have evil desire?—Guilty!

As we think of tomorrow we are painfully conscious of our inadequacy and our inability to live as we should. We almost give up to hopelessness and despair. Then we think of something else—the greatest something which can occupy a human mind. Let me give here a story of which Morris Wee reminds us.

As a young man, Dr. A. J. Cronin was in charge of a small hospital. One evening he performed an emergency operation on a little boy. It was a very delicate operation, and the doctor felt great relief when the little fellow breathed freely after it was over. He gave orders to the young nurse and went home filled with gratitude for the success. Late that night came a frantic call for the doctor. Everything had gone wrong, and the child was in desperate condition. When Dr. Cronin got to the bedside the boy was dead.

The nurse had become frightened and had neglected her duty. Dr. Cronin decided she should not be trusted again, and he wrote a letter to the board of health which would end her career as a nurse. He called her in and read the letter to her. She listened in shame and misery, saying nothing. Finally, Dr. Cronin asked, "Have you nothing to say?" She shook her head. She had no excuse to offer. Then she did speak, and this is what she said, "Give me another chance."

God gave us these ten rules to live by. Surely His heart has been grieved as again and again we violated them. We stand before Him in shame and misery, condemned without excuse. Not because we deserve it, but because of His infinite mercy, God gives us another chance. "For God so loved the world, that he gave his only begotten Son, that whosoever believeth in him should not perish, but have everlasting life" (John 3:16).

If you have not broken one of God's commandments,

I suppose you do not need the Saviour. But is there one among us who is innocent? We can only sing: "Just as I am, without one plea, but that Thy blood was shed for me." And as we look to the future we triumphantly say with the Apostle, "I can do all things through Christ which strengtheneth me" (Philippians 4:13). Through faith in Christ and obedience to His will our sins are forgiven and we have strength for victory tomorrow.

PART III

HOW TO TALK TO GOD

THE LORD'S PRAYER

After this manner therefore pray ye:
Our Father which art in heaven,
Hallowed be thy name.

Thy kingdom come. Thy will be done
in earth, as it is in heaven.

Give us this day our daily bread.

And forgive us our debts, as we forgive
our debtors.

And lead us not into temptation, but
deliver us from evil: For thine is
the kingdom, and the power, and the
glory, for ever. Amen. (Matthew 6:9-13)

1. NOT SAYING BUT PRAYING

THEY STOOD ONE DAY ON THE DECK OF A SHIP IN THE MIDST of a raging sea. They heard Him say quietly but with authority, "Peace, be still," and they were amazed as the winds and the waves obeyed His voice. He would speak to one paralyzed for many years, and they watched the man get up and walk.

They picked up twelve baskets full of left-overs after a crowd of 5,000 had eaten, yet all He had to begin with was a boy's lunch of five loaves and two fishes. They saw blind people, epileptics, lepers, even mentally deranged, healed with just a word from His lips. They saw the haunting burden of guilt drain out of human faces as He forgave. They heard Him speak as no man ever spoke. They felt the magnetism of His own life.

But their amazing wonder was changed into fearful responsibility when they heard Him say, "As my Father hath sent me, even so send I you." Surely they could not be expected to work His miracles. It was too much to ask of them. But they were filled with an awe-inspiring sense of possibility as He said to them: "Verily, verily, I say unto you, He that believeth on me, the works that I do shall he do also; and greater works than these shall he do; because I go unto my Father" (John 14:12).

Could it be true that such power could be theirs? He

said so, thus it was so. But how? Would He teach them His secrets? One day the answer burst upon them. There was one golden key to the power-house of God. Eagerly they said, "Lord, teach us to pray" (Luke 11:1). Learning to pray was the one, the only, secret they needed to know.

In response, Jesus gave them a prayer (Matthew 6:9-13). It can be said in one quarter of a minute, just fifteen seconds. Even for a large congregation of people to repeat it slowly takes only half a minute. Yet Jesus would spend half the night praying that same prayer. Today there are 500 million people who can say that prayer, but very few ever learn to pray it. The power comes, not in the saying, but in the praying of the prayer.

Praying is not saying words. Words merely form the frame on which the temple of thought is built. The power of the Lord's Prayer is not in the words, but rather in the pattern of thinking in which our minds are formed. The Bible tells us, "Be ye transformed by the renewing of your mind" (Romans 12:2). When our thoughts begin to flow in the channels of the Lord's Prayer our minds do become new, and we are transformed.

To the extent that we think the thoughts of Christ, to that same extent do we have the power of Christ. We remember how the king in Shakespeare's "Hamlet" miserably fails in prayer. In explanation, he says:

"My words fly up, my thoughts remain below;
Words without thoughts never to heaven go."

That's it! We, too, fail because our prayers are "words without thoughts."

88

2. OUR FATHER WHICH ART IN HEAVEN

"OUR FATHER WHICH ART IN HEAVEN," JESUS TELLS US TO pray. If we had only those six words we would have the Lord's Prayer. The other sixty words Jesus gave in the prayer are by way of explanation. Learn really to pray that first phrase and you need go no further.

The word "father" is a definition of God. For us it is an imperfect definition, because we as fathers are imperfect. A preacher who worked with boys in a slum area said he could not refer to God as a father. When those boys thought of father they pictured one who frequently was drunk and beat their mothers. We all put into that word the imperfections of our own fathers.

Thus Jesus could not use merely the term "Father." He must add, "which art in heaven." That phrase is not there to locate God or to tell us where God lives. Somehow, we have made up our minds that heaven is far distant. In one of our most beloved hymns, "The Old Rugged Cross," we sing, "He will call me some day to that home far away." And we think of God as being in that home far away. That is all wrong and not according to the teachings of Jesus. God is as near as the air you breathe.

Rather is "which art in heaven" a description of God. Heaven is synonymous with perfection. Jesus might have said, "Our perfect Father," and it would have been the same thing. And when you think of the term "father" immediately you think not of easy indulgence but of author-

89

ity. In the very act of recognizing a father you are making yourself a son. And the father has the right of command over his sons.

Therefore, you surrender your own will to His will. It is not what you want but what He wants that becomes your controlling thought. We recognize the fact that God has established a moral order. Man does not create his laws, he merely discovers God's laws. By obedience to those laws we learn with Dante, "His will is our peace."

On the other hand, to fail to recognize the sovereignty of God is to fail in all of life. The seal of one of the Waldensian churches pictures an anvil and a number of broken hammers, with the motto: "Hammer away, ye hostile hands! Your hammers break; God's anvil stands." So, until you can say "Father," you need not attempt to pray further.

However, father means more than ruler or lawgiver or judge. Father signifies a rule of love, it puts mercy into the very heart of judgment. Because love begets love, thus our response to God becomes not one of fear, but of true sonship. St. Paul said it well: "For ye have not received the spirit of bondage again to fear; but ye have received the Spirit of adoption, whereby we cry, Abba, Father" (Romans 8:15).

"Heavenly Father" means not only authority and love, it also means holiness. Once, as Isaiah walked into the church, he heard the seraphims singing, "Holy, holy, holy, is the Lord of hosts." When he saw the spotless purity of God he was convinced and convicted of his own unrighteousness to the point he cries, "Woe is me! for I am undone; because I am a man of unclean lips," and he falls before God in repentance and consecration (Isaiah 6:5).

Why is it we close our eyes when we pray? Perhaps the reason is to shut out the world in order to be able to give our complete attention to God. However, true prayer opens our eyes.

A great Hindu said: "Why are you so anxious to see God with your eyes closed? See Him with your eyes open—in the form of the poor, the starved, the illiterate, and the afflicted." To pray, "Father," means to recognize our sonship, but it also means to recognize our brotherhood.

A young man came in to see me recently. He had spent two years in prison. Sometimes we do not realize the blessings of society until we are shut away from it. He said to me, "I do not want much in life. I only want to belong again." "To belong," that is what we all want. But to pray, "Our Father," means to remove all boundaries and barriers and to make every one of us a child of God.

In this first phrase of the Lord's Prayer is summed up the Christian life. The word "Father" expresses our faith. Not only does it mean that we believe in a God, but also the very word describes Him. "In heaven" includes all our hopes. Meaning perfection, the word "heaven" signifies the quality of life toward which sincere Christians are striving. "Be ye therefore perfect," said Christ, "even as your Father which is in heaven is perfect" (Matthew 5:48).

Man is never satisfied with himself. He is ever striving upward and onward. He can bear the failures of the past and present because he hopes to do better tomorrow. When a friend was looking over the work of William W. Story, the famous sculptor, he asked: "For which of your carvings do you care the most?" To which the sculptor replied: "I care most for the statue I'm going to carve next."

The word "our" means all inclusive love. Without

that, prayer is futile. There is no such thing as a solitary religion, because unless we say "brother," we cannot say "Father." Ernest Crosby in his poem, "The Search," says it:

> No one could tell me where my soul might be;
> I sought for God, but God eluded me;
> I sought my brother out and found all three.

Faith—Hope—Love, they are all included.

How it would change my life to really pray, "Our Father which art in heaven." It would throw me on my knees in some Gethsemane in complete obedience to His will. It would lead me to sacrifice my life in serving and seeking to save my fellow man. Most important, it would bring God into my very soul.

Then, no matter what might happen, in complete confidence I could pray, even as my Lord prayed, "Father, into thy hands I commend my spirit" (Luke 23:46). Thus I would have the assurance that I could leave the results of my life in God's hands, knowing that even out of my seeming defeats in life would come glorious triumph. That out of the graves of my life would come resurrections and I would sing with the Apostle, "O death, where is thy sting? O grave, where is thy victory? . . . Thanks be to God, which giveth us the victory through our Lord Jesus Christ" (I Corinthians 15:55,57).

Rarely a week goes by that I do not conduct at least one burial service in West View Cemetery in Atlanta. Ten years ago now we laid my own father to rest there, and, before leaving, I usually go and stand at his grave and think about him. I always feel uplifted.

I think about how good he was to me. How that he

gave all he had in a material way to his children, not just food and clothes and the necessities of life. Also balls and bats and the things with which boys wanted to play. He was happy in making us happy. I think about each night he would pray for us, one by one. There is a recording of his voice in my mind as he prays, "Lord, bless Charles. May he grow up to be a good man." "Bless Stanley," he would say. "Bless John—Grace—Blanche—Sarah—Frances." He would have a special prayer for each of us.

Standing there at his grave, I think of his deep honesty, of his high standards. I think of his humility. He was very unpretentious, never seeking much for himself. Our parsonage was usually next door to the church, where day after day people came seeking help. I think of how he always shared what we had, never turning anybody away. Sometimes I forget about time as I stand there thinking about him.

So I feel I understand, at least in a very small way, something of what Jesus meant when He told us to pray, "Our Father." Again and again, our Lord would go out into the mountains alone to pray. He would often stay all night. On one occasion he even stayed forty days, forgetting time, even forgetting to eat. There in the quietness He would think about His Father.

And He tells us that is the way to pray, "Our Father which art in heaven." We are not asking God for something, instead we open the way for the inflow of God into us. Norman Vincent Peale tells of his first visit to the Grand Canyon. He met a man who had spent much time at the canyon, so he asked which trip he should take in order to see the most possible of the canyon.

The wise old man told him if he really wanted to see

the canyon he should not take any of the trips at all. Instead, he should come out early in the morning and take a seat on the rim, sit there and watch the morning pass into noontime and the noontime into afternoon, with the ever-changing colors gleaming across the great canyon. Then get a quick supper and return to watch the purple twilight come over the vast abyss. The old man said that if one runs around, he merely wears himself out and misses the beauty and greatness of it all.

Well, that is what the old prophet said about God in the long ago, "They that wait on the Lord shall renew their strength" (Isaiah 40:31). What does it mean to "wait on the Lord"? It means to think about God, though "think" is hardly the word. To meditate better expresses it, to contemplate is still better. Or as the Psalmist put it, "Be still, and know that I am God" (46:10).

H. G. Wells said, "Until a man has found God he begins at no beginning and works to no end." So you are not ready to pray until first your mind has been possessed by thoughts of God. For several years now I have watched hundreds of people kneel in prayer at the altar in the closing moments of the Sunday night service. Many have told me of amazing results of those prayers.

The reason why those altar prayers are so much more meaningful for many is because they come at the close of the service. For an hour or more the sacred building has been reminding them of the person of God. The hymns, the reading of the Bible, the sermon, the presence of other worshiping people, all work together to make one aware of the nearness of God. Then, when one kneels to pray his mind is properly conditioned, his thinking is Godly. Thus his prayer is natural and real. His words and his thoughts are the same.

94

"Our Father which art in heaven"—when those words become real to us we become quiet and confident. As the little verse expresses it:

> Said the Robin to the Sparrow,
> "I should really like to know
> Why these anxious human beings
> Rush around and worry so."
>
> Said the Sparrow to the Robin,
> "Friend, I think that it must be
> That they have no Heavenly Father,
> Such as cares for you and me."
>
> —ELIZABETH CHENEY

3. HALLOWED BE THY NAME

JESUS TEACHES US THAT THERE ARE SIX THINGS FOR WHICH man should pray. But before man can begin the other five petitions he must pray. "Hallowed be thy name." Once Moses was out on a hillside watching the sheep. He saw a bush on fire which continued to burn without burning up. After a time Moses went over to see about it.

Actually, God was in that bush, ready to reveal His will for Moses' life, but as Moses approached he heard a voice saying, "Put off thy shoes from off thy feet, for the place whereon thou standest is holy ground" (Exodus 3:5). The meaning of this is that before God speaks to man, man must have proper respect and reverence.

95

Many people never think of praying except in time of crisis. That is when we have a need which we ourselves cannot meet. And our prayers concern only ourselves, what we want God to do for us. That is why so few people really pray with power. Jesus says that first we must have God in our minds. To "hallow" means to respect and reverence.

But notice, Jesus does not tell us to hallow God's name. Rather is it a prayer, which means asking God to do something that we are unable to do. Thus we are asking God to hallow His own name. Profane man can do nothing for God until first God has done something for man. Suppose an artist, even the greatest artist of all time, said, "I shall go out and paint the sky." We would laugh at him. So man cannot hallow the name of God. If you tried to blacken the sky with a tar brush, you would succeed only in getting tar over yourself. The sky would remain as it is. So what does Jesus mean by this prayer?

The emphasis is not on the word "hallow" but on "name." The Bible is a book of names. Every name has a meaning, given to reveal the character of the person. For example, the name "Jesus" means "God is Salvation." Thus the angel said to Joseph: "Thou shalt call his name Jesus: for he shall save his people from their sins" (Matthew 1:21).

When Andrew brought his brother to Christ the Lord said, "Thou art Simon the son of Jona," which name means "shifting sand," which was descriptive of him. But under the influence of Christ he would become a different person. So Jesus says his name will be changed: "Thou shalt be called Cephas, which is by interpretation, A stone," something strong and unshakable (John 1:42).

To know a person's name was to know the person. Thus God's "name" means His nature revealed. So "Hallowed be thy name" really means, "Reveal thyself to me, O God." In the long ago Job asked, "Canst thou by searching find out God?" (Job 11:7). The answer is no. Man can know God only as God chooses to reveal Himself.

Walter de la Mare asks a question that we all sometimes ask. As he prays he wonders, "Is there anybody there?" Before you can pray you must be sure there is a Somebody to hear, and be conscious of His presence.

There are three ways—maybe four—in which God reveals Himself. First, in His marvelous creation. "The heavens declare the glory of God; and the firmament showeth his handiwork" (Psalm 19:1). That is the first revelation God made of Himself. We stand at the seashore and are moved by the boundless expanse before us. When we remember that He can hold all the seas in "the hollow of his hand" (Isaiah 40:12), then we see something of His power. Standing among great mountain peaks, His majesty is impressed upon us.

Jesus stood reverently before a wild "lily of the field" and saw the glory of God (Matthew 6:28,29). "Earth's crammed with heaven, and every common bush afire with God," sings Mrs. Browning. We look into the heavens and see the infiniteness of God, at a tiny snowflake and see His perfection. The sunset teaches us of His beauty.

Yet modern man is in danger of letting his own conceit blot out this revelation of God. Instead of praying for rain, we talk about making rain ourselves. We seed clouds, but who made the clouds? Jesus introduces us to a character much like ourselves. "The ground of a certain rich man brought forth plentifully; and he thought within himself, saying, What shall I do, because I have no room where to bestow my fruits? . . . I will pull down my barns, and build greater; and there will I bestow all my fruits and my goods" (Luke 12:16,18). I—I—I; My—My—My. There is no sense of God. God the creator he does not see.

Second, God reveals Himself through people. Through Moses we glimpse God's law, Amos showed us His justice, Hosea His love, and Micah His ethical standards. Someone was kind when we were sick, helped in time of trouble, was friendly when we were lonely. Someone we had wronged forgave in a spirit of love. In all such acts a little of God is revealed unto us. You better understand God because of the love of your mother, the consecrated life of some friend, the heroism of some Joan d'Arc. Corporate worship is so much more rewarding because we learn from each other.

God's supreme revelation of Himself is in Christ. "He that hath seen me hath seen the Father." As Harry Webb Farrington sang:

> *I know not how that Bethlehem's Babe*
> *Could in the Godhead be.*
> *I only know the manger Child*
> *Has brought God's life to me.*

> *I know not how that Calvary's cross*
> *A world of sin could free.*
> *I only know its matchless love*
> *Has brought God's love to me.*

> *I know not how that Joseph's tomb*
> *Could solve death's mystery;*

I only know a living Christ,
Our immortality.

As you read the four Gospels and see Jesus you begin to realize that you are actually seeing God.

One other way God reveals Himself. I have no name or explanation for it. We may call it the "still, small voice," or the impress of His spirit on us. But I can testify that there are times, perhaps rare times, when you feel you have received a direct word from Him. Samuel heard God directly.

As we know God, so can we pray, "Hallowed be thy name," that is "make us surer of Thee, O God, that we may understand Thee more fully." And as our minds are filled with God, as we steadily gaze upon Him, the little sins which so easily beset us lose their power over us, and we become both willing and able to hear and obey Him. That condition we must meet in order to pray with power.

4. THY KINGDOM COME

"THY KINGDOM COME" IS THE SECOND THING FOR WHICH Jesus told us to pray. The very word "kingdom" is offensive to Americans. "Democracy" is our word. We demand the right to govern ourselves. Kipling refers to us as a people among whom each man "dubs his dreary brethren Kings." Especially today do we rebel against dictators and totalitarianism. In fact, some of us assert the right of self-rule even to the point of dethroning God.

But we need to be reminded that in one sense God's kingdom has already come. His laws govern the universe with absolute authority. The scientist knows the law of God. He sees it in the precision of the cosmos. The physician will tell you there are certain laws of health. To obey them is to have health—to disobey them is to die. The psychiatrist understands that a man's pattern of thinking must be along right lines. To turn off the track is to become unbalanced. Even the sociologist teaches us that the good of one is the good of all. We are bound together in a common brotherhood, which is a law of God.

God established His kingdom on earth, which means His law and His rule. It is here right now. Whether we like it or not, His rule is upon us. As the prophet said in the long ago: "The soul that sinneth, it shall die" (Ezekiel 18:4).

We see the capitol building of our state. We know the governor and members of the legislature. We think of how man makes his laws. Yet any and every law of my state can be repealed or amended. There will be other governors and legislators.

Not so with the laws of God. I could rebel against God's law of gravitation and step out the window of a high building. But I would only destroy myself. I would not change the law. So I go down on an elevator. Is that not overcoming God's law with man's mechanical genius? No. Suppose the cable of the elevator breaks. It has happened. And the very fact that the elevator makers use such strong cables and regularly inspect them is a recognition of God's law and obedience to it.

This world is God's kingdom. It is under His sovereign rule and power, controlled by laws. However, in foolish disobedience, man rushes on to destroy himself. Will we ever come to our senses? Will we ever recognize the law of God to the point of surrender and obedience to it? There are many who say no. They are so depraved, so corrupted by egoism and so blinded by pride, that they cannot see the right way and have not the will to obey, even if they could.

Thus on every hand we hear destruction predicted for the world. We have eternal hell preached as our inescapable punishment. We are shouted at by would-be prophets who see no hope, but only the terror of an angry God's judgment. But Jesus said pray, "Thy kingdom come." Surely He believed not only in its possibility but in the actual event.

One night Jesus locked the door of His little carpenter's shop for the last time. He must be about His "Father's business." That business was to bring God's kingdom on earth. The text of His very first sermon was, "The kingdom of heaven is at hand" (Matthew 4:17). That was the one theme of His preaching all the way. He never lost His faith, and even on the resurrection side of the grave He talked to His disciples of the kingdom of God (Acts 1:3).

As we pray, "Thy kingdom come," it is well to underscore the word "come." It is so much easier to pray, "Thy kingdom go." It is not nearly as hard to pray for the conversion of Africa and to give offerings for missions as it is to face up honestly to the sins of our own lives, to repent and change our ways.

It is easier to crusade piously for world peace than it is to forgive someone who has done us wrong or whom we have wronged. David Livingstone sought out the savage with the word of God, but first he dedicated himself. Even the last day of his life he wrote in his diary, "My Jesus, my King, my Life, my All, I again dedicate my whole self to Thee."

There is a verse of Scripture that literally haunts me. I have the blessed privilege of preaching to many people. During the very week I am writing these words I am visiting in Columbia, the capital city of South Carolina, preaching in one of the largest churches of the state. Each night the great auditorium is being filled and many are being turned away. Yet there is something much harder than preaching to others. St. Paul said: "But I keep under my body, and bring it into subjection: lest that by any means, when I have preached to others, I myself should be a castaway" (I Cor. 9:27). If the greatest Christian preacher of all time was in danger of becoming a castaway, how much more so is it true for me.

"Thy kingdom come." It means that I look into my own heart and plead for God's cleansing power. It means that I bow before Him in faith and obedience.

Archibald Rutledge told the story of meeting a Negro turpentine worker whose faithful dog had died a few moments earlier in a great forest fire because he would not desert his master's dinner pail, which he had been told to watch. With tears in his face, the old Negro said: "I always had to be careful what I tol' him to do, 'cause I knowed he'd do it." That is what this prayer means.

Jesus said, "The kingdom of heaven is like unto a merchant man, seeking goodly pearls: who, when he had found one pearl of great price, went and sold all that he had, and bought it" (Matthew 13:45,46). The pearls he sold meant a lifetime of labor. They represented all he had. Yet the one pearl was worth all else. So, to really pray, "Thy kingdom come," means I am willing to surrender everything I possess in order to possess God. God demands our all or nothing at all.

It is so much easier for me to talk about the sins of the world, the corruption of government, for instance, or the evils of liquor, or the filthy literature and motion pictures, or the honky-tonks around town, or the heathens in China. But before I pray about where God's kingdom is needed, first let it come to me.

Jonathan Edwards, one of the most effective preachers America ever knew, so prayed. He said, "I go out to preach with two propositions in mind. First, every person ought to give his life to Christ. Second, whether or not anyone else gives Him his life, I will give Him mine."

The apostle said, "Let all bitterness, and wrath, and anger, and clamor, and evil speaking, be put away from you, with all malice: And be ye kind one to another, tenderhearted, forgiving one another, even as God for Christ's sake hath forgiven you" (Ephesians 4:31,32). That is what the coming of God's kingdom means for us, and when it comes, then we can spread it forth with power. Unrighteous people are not very powerful crusaders for a righteous world. As the spiritual tells us: "It ain't my brother, it ain't my sister, it's me, O Lord, standing in the need of prayer."

"Thy kingdom come." When that prayer is answered, then we shall have no doubt of the power of God's kingdom to cover the earth.

5. THY WILL BE DONE IN EARTH, AS IT IS IN HEAVEN

To PRAY WITH POWER, JESUS TEACHES US WE MUST FIRST get God in our minds and recognize His sovereignty. We must pray, "Thy will be done." Right there many people hesitate, lose their nerve, and turn away from God. I think I know why.

When I was studying psychology in college I worked out a number of word tests which I would use on my congregations. For example, say to a person the word "Christmas" and ask that person the first word which comes into his mind. I would get such answers as Santa Claus, decorations, gifts, etc. Rarely would Christ be mentioned. So I would conclude we had commercialized and paganized the Lord's birthday. I think the test was valid, with some limitations.

Well, let's try it on ourselves. I will name a phrase and check your first thought. "Will of God." What does that bring to your mind? The death of a loved one, or some great disaster, or severe suffering from some incurable disease, or some hard sacrifice. Most people will think of some dark picture in relation to the will of God.

Perhaps one cause is our Lord's prayer in Gethsemane, "Nevertheless not my will, but thine be done" (Luke 22:42). And from His surrender to God's will we see Christ walking up Calvary and being nailed to a cross. So God's will and crosses come to be synonymous terms for us.

104

However, we can go back further. There was Job. He lost his wealth, his children were killed, he suffered in body, and his wife deserted him. Job associated all those disasters with God, so he says, "The Lord gave, and the Lord hath taken away; blessed be the name of the Lord" (Job 1:21). So, when our hearts are broken we say "It is the Lord's will." Naturally we shrink from such a will.

It seems to be a general belief that the will of God is to make things distasteful for us, like taking bad tasting medicine when we are sick, or going to the dentist. Yet we think we would be much happier if we disregarded God's will. We never say, "No, I forever turn my back on God's will." But we do say, "For the time being I will back my own judgment and follow my own will."

Somebody needs to tell us that sunrise is also God's will. There is the time of harvest, the harvest which will provide food and clothes for us, without which life could not be sustained on earth. God ordered the seasons, they are His will. In fact, the good things in life far outweigh the bad. There are more sunrises than cyclones.

I live comfortably during the winter in an automatically steam-heated house. Long before I was born God stored up the gas in the ground which is now being piped into my home for my good. I might say that cold winter freezes are God's will, but I must also know that the warmth God has provided is also His will. Whether you shrink from His will or gratefully surrender to it depends on how you look at it.

Jesus said, "Thy will be done in earth, as it is in heaven." "As in heaven," He said. What do you think of when the word "heaven" comes to your mind? You think of peace, plenty, perfect joy, the absence of pain and suffering and tears. John saw it all and recorded his vision in Revelation 21. That is exactly what we want here and now in our own lives.

Jesus says that is God's will for us.

Before you can pray, "Thy will be done," you must believe it is the best and happiest way. However, sometimes we surrender to the immediate, while God considers life as a whole. For example, here are two boys in school. The will of the teacher is that they spend hours in hard studying. One of the boys rebels against the unpleasant work. He wants to be happy, so he goes to a picture show. Maybe he quits school altogether to go his carefree way.

The other boy sticks to his studies, difficult though they may be. Look at those same two boys ten or twenty years later. The carefree boy is now bound and limited by his own ignorance. He endures hardships and embarrassments caused by his lack of training. The other boy is freer, happier, and finds life easier and more rewarding because he was properly prepared.

There was Joseph, the darling of his father Jacob's heart. Home was for him a place of great joy. But jealousy welled up in his brothers, who put Joseph in a dark well, and later sold him into slavery. Later those same brothers stood before him in need. Joseph said to them: "Be not grieved, nor angry with yourselves, that ye sold me hither: for God did send me before you to preserve life" (Genesis 45:5).

Surely Joseph's way was hard. But he kept his faith, never giving up, and at the end he could look back and see, as we read in "Hamlet," "There's a divinity that shapes our ends." Out of the surrender of our Lord in

Gethsemane did come a cross, but beyond the cross lay an empty tomb and a redeemed world.

Sometimes it is not God who leads us through deep valleys and dark waters. It may be man's ignorance and folly. But even then we can feel His presence, for out of our mistakes God can make something beautiful. God did not bring Job's tragedies. But because of Job's faith God could use those tragedies for Job's final good. It is wonderful what God can do with a broken heart when we give Him all the pieces.

Not only is God's way the best and happiest, it is also within our reach. Many shrink from God's will because of a fear that God will ask them to do more than they can do. There was the man of one talent who buried it in the earth. In explaining his failure, his not even trying, he said to his master: "Lord, I knew thee that thou art an hard man . . . and I was afraid, and went and hid thy talent in the earth" (Matthew 25:24,25).

He was afraid of unreasonable demands by his master. He felt that even his best could not please his master. There are some things we cannot do. Not many of us can be great artists. Conspicuous leadership is beyond the reach of most. We could list thousands of things we cannot do.

But of one thing we can be sure, we can do the will of God. Moses thought he couldn't. When God told him to lead the children of Israel out of bondage he made excuses. He sincerely felt it was beyond his abilities. But he did it. With complete faith and confidence, you can pray "Thy will be done," because God is a loving father who knows His children better than they know themselves. He wants our best, but He expects no more.

To pray, "Thy will be done," is really an enlistment

for action. In 1792 William Carey preached a sermon on the text: "Enlarge the place of thy tent, and let them stretch forth the curtains of thine habitations: spare not, lengthen thy cords, and strengthen thy stakes" (Isaiah 54:2).

It was one of the most influential sermons ever preached on this earth, because the result was the birth of the Baptist Missionary Society, the story of which a hundred books could not begin to tell. In that sermon Carey made his famous statement: "Expect great things from God, attempt great things for God."

But here is the important point. He not only preached about missions, he gave up all he had and went himself to India as a missionary. He prayed literally, "in earth as it is in heaven." He meant the whole earth and he dedicated his life in answer to his own prayer.

Recently a letter came asking me to pray that no child would ever again be crippled by polio. The letter quotes the Bible: "It is not the will of your Father which is in heaven, that one of these little ones should perish" (Matthew 18:14). Having three children of my own, certainly I can pray that polio be eliminated.

And I feel certain we can have that prayer answered any time we want. But we put into our national budget fifty billion dollars for armament. When we consider polio we talk about the "March of Dimes." Who knows but that if the money we have spent on atomic bombs had been used in medical research, we would not now have the answer not only for polio but also for cancer, arthritis, and many other diseases.

We feel compelled to maintain our vast program of defense. Yet whose fault is it? If we had spent on Christian missions in Japan the cost of one battleship which the Japanese sank at Pearl Harbor, we might never have had that war. If we had maintained a Christian spirit in Germany after World War I, Hitler might never have been heard of.

Actually, God's will is on earth. It is operating in your very life. For example, you did not decide in what century you would be born. You were not free to choose who your parents would be. The color of your skin, your sex, your physical appearance, all were decided by a higher will, God's will.

And God's will is in operation in our lives. There is a purpose for your life. I believe no person is an accident. Before you were born on the earth you existed in the mind of God. You can rebel against God, but ultimately you will be totally defeated. You can endure life as it comes, and find no joy and peace in it. Or you can choose the will of God and make His will your will.

As Tennyson put it: "Our wills are ours, we know not how; our wills are ours, to make them thine."

How can I know the will of God for my life? Many will never know, because God does not reveal Himself to triflers. No one can walk into His holy presence on hurrying feet. If you merely pray, "Lord, this is my will, I hope you will approve," you are wasting your breath. Only those who sincerely want God's will, and have faith enough in Him to dedicate themselves to His will, can ever know it. To pray, "Lord, show me Thy will. If I like it I will accept it," is a futile prayer. You must accept it before you know it. Whether or not you can do that depends on what opinion you have of God.

To the sincere, God reveals His will in many ways.

Often we learn through the process we call insight. A psychiatrist said to me once, "Either a person has insight or he hasn't. It isn't something which can be learned." But it is something which God can give.

I have talked with people who have baffling problems. Maybe they have tossed many weary hours trying to sleep, but could not because of a problem. In the quietness of the pastor's study we have talked about God and His love and concern for us. After a prayer, we talked about the problem. And not once, but many times, I have seen a light on their faces, as suddenly the answer came, a solution came to mind. I say God gave them insight. Sometimes it is called the "inner light."

God may reveal His will through the advice of others, through circumstances, through the experiences of history, through the discovery of His laws by scientific investigation, through the voice of His Church. Certainly we see His will as we study the life and teachings of Jesus.

I have a little radio that I carry in my bag. At home I can hear any station in Atlanta I turn to. But if I get too far away the voice of the station is blotted out. It is the same radio—the station is broadcasting with the same power. But I have gone too far away. Many miss God's voice because they are too far away from Him.

The assurance that you are within the will of God does more to eliminate the fears and worries of life than any other one thing. I quote Dante: "In His will is our peace." Surrender to His will takes the dread out of tomorrow. We know, absolutely we know, that if we do His will today, tomorrow will be according to His will. I am not a fatalist, instead I can say with the Psalmist, "I have not seen the righteous forsaken" (37:25). Obedience to His will today means that God assumes the responsibility for our tomorrow.

So, Jesus teaches us that the first three petitions of our prayer must be with our eyes fixed firmly on God. There is a place in prayer to talk about our own needs, and our Lord assures us it is right to pray for ourselves, but first God must fill our minds before we come to our own problems. Then we are ready to talk about what we want Him to do for us.

6. GIVE US THIS DAY OUR DAILY BREAD

IN THE MIDDLE OF THE LORD'S PRAYER THERE IS A DISTINCT division. You see it in the pronouns. In the first three petitions we are taught to say "Thy," "Thy name," "Thy kingdom," "Thy will." But in the last three petitions are "us" and "our." First, we think of God, then we can rightfully think of ourselves.

And the very first petition our Lord permits us to pray for ourselves is the one we really want to pray. In fact, it is the one we must pray if we plan to stay alive. "Give us this day our daily bread." By that He means simply the physical necessities of life.

Many of the early church fathers, such as Jerome, Origen, and Augustine taught that this petition was for the same bread which Jesus refers to when He says, "I am the bread of life" (John 6:35). They felt it was wrong to pray

111

for material blessings. And that idea persists to this day.

But why try to spiritualize this petition? After all, even a saint must eat. Even our very prayers would die on our lips if we did not have food to sustain our bodies. Jesus preached to the people, He healed the sick, He forgave their sins, and He also used his marvelous power to feed them real bread.

Study our Lord's life. You will see He knew something about the everyday struggle to make ends meet. He knew the meaning of the widow's two mites, what a disaster the loss of a coin might be, wearing clothes which were patched. He knew about shopping in the grocery store to try to stretch a budget to feed the family. He talks about the housewife who must buy two birds which sold for a penny.

Even on the resurrection side of the grave our Lord was concerned with bread. We see Him walking home with two of His friends on that first Easter Sunday. He spoke hope to their hearts and He also took time to sit at the table with them. In fact, the Bible says, "He took bread, and blessed it, and brake, and gave to them" (Luke 24:30).

In the gray dawn of the morning we see Him on the seashore. His disciples had been fishing all night. Now they were coming in, and the Lord was prepared for them. What did He prepare? A prayer meeting? They needed prayer. A majestic and overwhelming revelation of Himself? They had lost faith in Him. No, He prepared breakfast.

The risen, resplendent Christ cooking breakfast! Though His feet were bruised, He walked over a rocky beach to gather firewood. Though His hands were nail-pierced, He cleaned fish. He knew that the fishermen would be hungry.

He knows we have groceries to buy, rent or payments to make on our houses, clothes that are necessary, expenses for the children in school, bills of every sort to meet. Not only that, He knows we have desires and wants beyond our bare necessities. We are not wild beasts. We want some of the pleasant things of life.

Much better than we, He knew that the body and the soul are an inseparable unity. Just as worry and fear can affect the body and make one sick, so one's physical condition can affect a man's outlook on life, his religious faith, his moral conduct.

The God who made our bodies is concerned about the needs of our bodies and He is anxious for us to talk with Him about our physical needs.

Every morning the sun rises to warm the earth. If it were to fail to shine for just one minute, all life on the earth would die. The rains come to water the earth. There is fertility in the soil, life in the seeds, oxygen in the air. The providence of God is about us in unbelievable abundance every moment. But so often we just take it for granted.

Dr. John Witherspoon was a great American and a man of God. He was one of the signers of the Declaration of Independence and president of the College of New Jersey which later became Princeton. He lived about two miles from the college and drove over in his buggy each day.

One morning a neighbor came excitedly into his study and said, "Dr. Witherspoon, you must join me in giving thanks to God for His providence in saving my life.

As I was driving this morning the horse ran away and the buggy was smashed to pieces on the rocks, but I escaped unharmed."

"Why," answered Dr. Witherspoon, "I can tell you a far more remarkable providence than that. I have driven over that road hundreds of times. My horse never ran away, my buggy never was smashed, I was never hurt. God's providence has been for me even more remarkable than it has been for you."

All of us know so well Maltbie D. Babcock's little verse:

> Back of the loaf is the snowy flour,
> And back of the flour the mill,
> And back of the mill is the wheat and the shower,
> And the sun and the Father's will.

The same is true of everything you have—the new television set you enjoy, or the nice car in which you take such great pride, or the home in which you live, or the clothes you are now wearing. All of those things come from the earth which God made. He put those things within our reach because He knew we would want them and would enjoy them. Long before you were born, God answered your prayer for material blessings. "Give us this day our daily bread" is a prayer that has truly been answered. It is also a recognition of what He has already done. I like to read that story of Jesus in the wilderness. Matthew tells us there were five thousand people with Him (14:21). They were hungry, and the Lord wanted them fed. The disciples surveyed the situation, and all the food they could find was a little boy's lunch of five loaves and two small fishes.

The disciples felt this was too little with which to

bother. With such meager resources, there was no need to try. But watch the Lord's actions. No complaint from Him about not having more. Instead, the first thing He did was give thanks for it. Then He started using what He had. He began breaking and passing the food out.

To the astonishment of all, what He had was enough to feed everyone. In fact, they had more than they needed, and there were twelve baskets of food left over. The people were so amazed that immediately they tried to take Him by force and make him a king (John 6:5-15).

If today we would begin being thankful for what we have, and use it as best we can, God would give us insight as to how we could multiply what we have to cover every need of our lives, and have a lot left over. We would be so blessed that we would fall before Him as our Lord and King.

7. AND FORGIVE US OUR DEBTS, AS WE FORGIVE OUR DEBTORS

JESUS GIVES US SIX PETITIONS TO MAKE. THREE CONCERN God, and three are for ourselves. All six of them are of supreme importance, yet there is one of the six on which He turns the spotlight. He does not find it necessary to emphasize that we pray that God's name be hallowed, or that God's kingdom come, or that His will be done, vital as those are.

He does not emphasize our need for bread, yet without

bread we would all die. But after the Lord's Prayer is completed, our Lord feels He should turn back and lift one petition out for special comment. "And forgive us our debts, as we forgive our debtors" is the prayer He spotlights. He says, "But if ye forgive not men their trespasses, neither will your Father forgive your trespasses" (Matthew 6:15).

It isn't that God forgives on an exchange basis. Our forgiveness of others is not a condition of God's forgiveness of us. Rather is it a condition of our ability to receive the forgiveness of God. We are told by Shakespeare, "The quality of mercy is not strain'd, it droppeth as the gentle rain from heaven." But I could cover a plant with a sheet of iron and the rain could not get to it. So, I can surround my soul with an unforgiving spirit and completely block the forgiving mercy of God.

A wrong spirit toward another person may or may not hurt him, but it is certain to destroy my own soul. Booker T. Washington understood it when he said, "I will not permit any man to narrow and degrade my soul by making me hate him."

I remember a scene from "Amos and Andy." There was a big man who would slap Andy across the chest whenever they met. Finally, Andy got enough of it and said to Amos, "I am fixed for him. I put a stick of dynamite in my vest pocket and the next time he slaps me he is going to get his hand blown off." Andy had not realized that at the same time his own heart would be blown out. The dynamite of hatred may inflict some injury on someone else and also blow out our own heart.

The words "forgiving" and "forgiven" are inseparable twins. They go together. They are never separated. At the death of Queen Caroline Lord Chesterfield said a sad thing: "And unforgiving, unforgiven dies."

On the cross our Lord prays, "Father, forgive them; for they know not what they do" (Luke 23:34). Often what we deplore is the innocent act of some person. But for us there is an even more important reason for not holding a grudge: "for *we* know not." If we understood the person, usually our judgments would not be so harsh.

With our limited understanding of each other, it is a fearful thing to set ourselves up as a judge. The Bible says, "Vengeance is mine; I will repay, saith the Lord" (Romans 12:19). If we are wise we will leave that business to God. Somewhere I read these lines:

Has God deserted Heaven,
And left it up to you,
To judge if this or that is right,
And what each one should do?

I think He's still in business,
And knows when to wield the rod,
So when you're judging others,
Just remember, you're not—God.

"As we forgive," He told us to pray.

A couple had gone to an orphanage to adopt a child. One little fellow particularly appealed to them. They talked to him about all the things they would give him—clothes, toys, a good home. None of these things seemed to appeal to the boy much. So finally they asked him, "What do you want most?" He replied, "I just want somebody to love me."

That is what we all want. Deep in every human heart

is a hunger for love. Loneliness is a cross for more people than we realize. Yet people are hard to love. They have so many faults, they say things they shouldn't, many have antagonistic and unattractive spirits. Yet Jesus told us to pray, "Forgive as we forgive." This is the only petition He emphasized. Maybe it is the hardest one to say.

"For if you forgive not men their trespasses"—debts—sins—! Either of those words could be used, maybe all three better express what our Lord had in mind. Debts suggest failure to discharge obligations, not merely financial. There are also such debts as the debts of friendship, citizenship, etc.

Trespasses indicates the unlawful use of another's property. We see signs, "No Trespassing," and we know that the sign means to keep off. Our friends also trespass on our time, they trespass on our name and do it harm when they talk about us wrongfully. In many ways do friends trespass on us.

Sin indicates vice and wrong conduct. And we see a lot in our friends. In fact, the more you study the faults of your friends, the harder it becomes to offer this prayer, "as we forgive others." And sometimes we invest our love in friends only to be bitterly disappointed.

Sometimes we might feel like Sir Walter Raleigh, who just a few hours before his death, wrote his wife: "To what friend to direct thee I know not, for mine have left me in the true time of trial." Some people have been so deeply hurt that they cannot feel that Tennyson was right when he said:

I hold it true, whate'er befall,
I feel it, when I sorrow most;

'Tis better to have loved and lost,
Than never to have loved at all.

But notice carefully that Jesus said, "Forgive us our debts." He directs our attention first to our own debts—trespasses—sins. The faults of those about us are also in us. Maybe not exactly the same ones, but probably worse ones. He did not tell us to pray, "Forgive us *if* we have sinned." There is no *if* about it.

Let us honestly ask ourselves some questions and answer them: "What is my worst failure? That is, wherein have I not lived up to my obligations? Second, what is one way I have mistreated another person? Third, what is one sin I have committed?" Each of us has some answer for each of those questions. We all stand convicted.

But, also, do our friends have an answer for those questions? They, too, are guilty. Now, the supreme point is: If you will be willing to forgive them, then you will be able to receive God's forgiveness of you. It seems to be a good bargain for me. How about you?

8. AND LEAD US NOT INTO TEMPTATION, BUT DELIVER US FROM EVIL

Our Lord gives us three prayers to pray for ourselves. One is for the present, "Give us this day our daily bread." One looks both to the past and to the present, "Forgive us our sins." The third prayer looks to the future. As to our need to pray for bread and for forgiveness we are in agreement, but most of us take a view different from that of our Lord as to the prayer we should pray for tomorrow.

As we look to the future what is it we need to pray about? What do we fear and shrink from the most? For some the answer is sickness, so we ask God to keep us well, we are interested in preventive medicine, we take out sick and hospitalization insurance. We fear poverty, so we save for the rainy days. Others fear suffering. We worry about the possibility of being hurt.

We fear unpopularity and criticism, we fear old age, we fear death. But when Christ tells us what to pray about for the future, He mentions not one of these things. The one thing we need to pray about for the future is the possibility of doing wrong. The one fear we should have above all fears is that in the midst of temptation we shall slip.

But we take less seriously our Lord's prayer for the future than we take any of the other five petitions. We are not afraid of temptation. In fact, we are so confident of being able to command our own selves that we make temptation a constant companion.

There is an old story of a man who had been the victim of strong drink but had reformed and apparently was the conqueror of his evil habit. However, when he drove into town, he continued to hitch his horse at the post in front of the town saloon. Eventually he fell into his old ways again. Had he had a healthy fear of temptation he would have changed his hitching post.

Temptation most often comes first as thoughts. In the secret places of our minds we dramatize and act out the thoughts. We read books that describe wickedness, we play with emotional dynamite as if it were a harmless toy. We get ourselves into dangerous situations and enjoy being there. We keep the wrong company. When we go about work or pleasure some enticing voice may whisper, "Brother, lend me your soul." We might hesitate to give away a dime, even if we have a pocketful of coins, but we risk our souls though we know it may be for eternity. When it is temptation we face we are foolishly brave.

Not so with Jesus. He tells us to fear the temptation of the morrow more than any other thing. Our very strength is our greatest weakness, because the overconfidence in our strength leads to our downfall. We are afraid of our weaknesses and guard against them. But we take chances with our strengths, and that is where we lose. "Wherefore let him that thinketh he standeth take heed lest he fall" (I Cor. 10:12).

What is temptation? First, it is an inducement to evil. Read the third chapter of Genesis and you see a story that has been repeated in some form in the life of every person who has come after Adam and Eve.

The serpent says to Eve, "Hath God said, Ye shall not eat of every tree in the garden?" Eve replies, "All except one. If we eat of that one we shall die." The serpent tells her it will not hurt her. "In fact, if you eat of that tree you will know more, you will have a larger and freer life."

Here her inclinations began to struggle with her reason and conscience. The "Thou-shalt-not" of God and the bright alluring promise of forbidden pathways came in conflict. Thus temptation was set up.

Second, temptation means a test or a trial. It is like

a fork in the roadway of life, where one must decide the direction to take, an action to carry out, a character to be. A mother whose son has been killed may be tempted to become bitter and harsh. One who is facing a difficult life situation may be tempted to escape by getting drunk.

One who is destined to a bed of suffering or the chair of an invalid may be tempted to self-pity. When someone has treated us unfairly there is the temptation to hate, spite, or resentment. One who has prospered is tempted to vanity and self-love. The successful is tempted to seek undue power.

When he was a boy in school Napoleon wrote an essay on the dangers of ambition. Yet his own ambition wrecked his life. Moses was noted for his meekness. In fact, the Bible says he was the meekest man on earth (Numbers 12:3). Yet, in a moment, when he tried to usurp the power of God by striking the rock, he lost his chance to enter the Promised Land. Simon Peter was noted for his impulsive courage. Yet it was through failure of his greatest strength that he denied his Lord.

A man is no stronger than his weakest moment, and every man has an Achilles' heel, a point of vulnerability. We cannot escape temptation because we are endowed with freedom of choice. And since no person has an iron will, every one is in danger of falling. We can choose between good and evil, between being true and false, between being brave and cowardly, between being generous and selfish. And the very freedom of choice becomes in itself temptation.

Many stumble at the interpretation of this petition, feeling that God would not lead one of His children into temptation. But God is concerned with the creation of character, and to create character He gives us freedom of choice. Otherwise we would be mere puppets.

Life would be much simpler if we had no such freedom. Thomas Henry Huxley once declared: "If some great Power would agree to make me think always what is true and do what is right on condition of being turned into a sort of clock, I should instantly close with the bargain. The only freedom I care about is the freedom to do right; the freedom to do wrong I am ready to part with." But one freedom requires the other freedom, thus our temptation.

God gave to each of us a free will, yet the very possession of our freedom should so frighten us that in every possible way we should throw safeguards around it. We should be very afraid of any circumstance that might mean our downfall.

Jesus tells us: "If thy right hand offend thee, cut it off" (Matthew 5:30). He may mean those words literally, for certainly it would be better to lose one's hand than to lose one's soul. However, I think He means by the hand the work of the hand—"Whatsoever thy hand findeth to do . . ." If your daily job brings you into situations which tempt you, better for one to give up the job even at the cost of sacrifice.

Again He says, "If thy right eye offend thee, pluck it out" (Matthew 5:29). Probably what He means by "thy eye" is the things you have your eye set on—your goals and ambitions. One can be so set on success, social or material, that he reaches the point where he demands "success at any price." If the direction of your life is a peril to your soul, better to try another road.

Elizabeth Barrett Browning understood it when she said:

I was too ambitious in my deed,
And thought to distance all men in success,
Till God came on me, marked the place, and said,
"Ill-doer, henceforth keep within this line,
Attempting less than others"—and I stand,
And work among Christ's little ones, content.

"Lead us not into temptation" is a prayer that makes us look at our choices, beyond our goals to the final destination of the road we would travel.

This is a prayer that can be answered and is answered in many ways. Sometimes it is answered by God's direct providence by what we call coincidence. Why is it you missed getting a certain job or opportunity? Maybe it was God intervening. At times this prayer is answered by what we call insight. In certain hard moments of decision we feel deep inside the right course to take.

Most of all is this prayer answered by the inner strength which God gives to all who sincerely desire it. In despair we sometimes throw up our hands. We feel caught in an entanglement of circumstances, or by the chains of some habit, or by our own inherent weakness. We say, "What's the use? I cannot do better." But when we sincerely desire to rise above our temptations and look to God for deliverance a new inner strength becomes ours, a new spirit of confidence rises within us.

One of the most sublime verses in the Bible is tucked away in the little book of Jude: "Now unto him that is able to keep you from falling, and to present you faultless before the presence of his glory with exceeding joy" (verse 24). You begin to realize you are made for victory instead of defeat, that you are to overcome evil rather than to be overcome by it, and triumphantly you declare with the Apostle: "I can do all things through Christ which strengtheneth me" (Philippians 4:13).

The biggest lie of the devil is that we have to sin. "After all, you are human," he says, and thereby our high resolves are destroyed. We surrender and quit the struggle. One takes a very different view when he becomes acquainted with a power beyond human power. "I can do all things through Christ which strengtheneth me." That is a tremendously powerful truth, once we possess it.

There is a little story we read as children about the little engine climbing the hill. As it puffed and struggled it kept saying, "I think I can, I think I can, I think I can." Nothing is ever accomplished by the person who says, "I think I cannot," or "It is beyond me." Just to say, "I can," is to gain immediate power. But to add two words and say, "I can in Him," "I can in Him," is to multiply your power many fold.

I read recently of an experiment made by a psychologist. We are familiar with those gripping machines. You put in a penny and try your grip. Three men tried their grip, with no suggestion from the psychologist, and the average grip was 101 pounds. Then the three were hypnotized and the psychologist told each, "You cannot grip, because you are weak." Under the power of that suggestion their average grip fell from 101 pounds to only 29 pounds.

With the three men still under the power of hypnosis, the psychologist told them to grip again, but this time he told them, "Now you can grip." Their strength was five times greater when they said, "I can," than it was when they said, "I cannot."

Study the lives of those we call saints, those who have attained unusual spiritual power, and you will find their secret right at this point. They sinned, but they never surrendered to sin. They never accepted failure as final. They never ceased to look forward with confidence. They kept saying, "I can in Him." And to the utmost of their power was added His power.

The same power is available for any one of us. You may look into a past of shame and defeat, but I tell you that you can look into a future of peace and victory. "Only believe, only believe all things are possible, only believe." That is more than just a little chorus. It is the Christian faith.

What amazing confidence did our Lord have in us! C. F. Andrews reminds us of an old legend that tells us that when Jesus returned to heaven He was asked by an angel: "What have you left behind to carry out the work?" Jesus answered: "A little band of men and women who love me." "But what if they fail when the trial comes? Will all you have done be defeated?" "Yes," said Jesus, "if they fail, all I have done will be defeated."

"Is there nothing more?" "No," said Jesus, "there is nothing more." "What then?" Jesus quietly replied, "They will not fail."

With a confidence like that as we face tomorrow, we can triumphantly declare: "For thine is the kingdom, and the power, and the glory, forever. Amen." We see the complete victory of God in our own lives and our world.

PART IV

THE KEYS TO THE KINGDOM

*And he opened his mouth, and taught them,
saying,*

*Blessed are the poor in spirit: for theirs
is the kingdom of heaven.*

*Blessed are they that mourn: for they shall
be comforted.*

*Blessed are the meek: for they shall inherit
the earth.*

*Blessed are they which do hunger and thirst
after righteousness: for they shall be filled.*

*Blessed are the merciful: for they shall obtain
mercy.*

*Blessed are the pure in heart: for they shall
see God.*

*Blessed are the peacemakers: for they shall be
called the children of God.*

*Blessed are they which are persecuted for right-
eousness' sake: for theirs is the kingdom
of heaven.*

*Blessed are ye, when men shall revile you, and
persecute you, and shall say all manner of
evil against you falsely, for my sake.*

*Rejoice, and be exceeding glad: for great is
your reward in heaven: for so persecuted
they the prophets which were before you.*

MATTHEW 5:2-12

1. BLESSED ARE THE POOR IN SPIRIT: FOR THEIRS IS THE KINGDOM OF HEAVEN

FREDERICK WILLIAM IV OF PRUSSIA ONCE VISITED A SCHOOL and asked the children some questions. Pointing to the stone in his ring, a flower in his button-hole, and a bird that flew past the window, he asked to what kingdom each of them belonged. The children gave him the right answers: the mineral, the vegetable, and the animal kingdoms.

Then he asked, "To what kingdom do I belong?" That is really the supreme question facing every man. For some men the answer is the animal kingdom, because they live on the appetite level, and are controlled by their passions and physical desires. But most people rise above the animal level. They have a sense of right and wrong, a feeling of duty and decency, some ideals and purposes.

However, some rise to an even higher kingdom. No one can think of Christ as being animal. Though He took the form of man, the word "human" is insufficient to describe Him. Christ was divine. He belonged to a kingdom beyond the kingdoms of this world. The Bible tells us we can enter jointly with Him into His kingdom: "The Spirit itself beareth witness with our spirit, that we are the children of God: and if children, then heirs; heirs of God and joint-heirs with Christ" (Romans 8:16,17).

We can belong to the Kingdom of God! That is a thrilling fact and gives to every life a thrilling mission. Recently someone asked me this question, "What do you want ten years from now?" I might answer that I want to be preaching, to be helping to build some church, some degree of comfort and security, to see my children becoming established in life. There are so many things I want.

But if I know my heart, as I think I do, I want, above all things, to belong to the Kingdom of God. Well, Jesus gave us eight keys to God's kingdom. The first key is poverty. Right off, we are tempted to say, "I qualify so far as poverty is concerned. Let's look at the second key."

But are you really poor? So far as material possessions are concerned, we are all poor. Even the man with a million dollars does not have enough to create one loaf of bread or to buy one moment of real contentment or to keep his soul out of hell. Yes, you are poor.

Also, the ten spies who went into the Promised Land were poor. Whimperingly they reported: "And there we saw giants . . . and we were in our own sight as grasshoppers" (Numbers 13:33). The man with one talent was poor. He buried his talent in the ground. There are a lot of people who do not have the courage really to amount to anything. They are very poor, indeed.

On the other hand, one might possess a certain cocksureness and yet be very poor. Peter typifies that type of poverty when he says: "Though all men shall be offended because of thee, yet will I never be offended" (Matthew 26:33). He was not poor in spirit, yet he was poor, as it was proved when the testing time came.

The first key to God's Kingdom is another type of poverty.

Two men went up to the Temple to pray. One said, "God, I thank thee, that I am not as other men are." He listed all his good qualities and was quite satisfied. He had a good eye for himself, a bad eye for his fellow men, and no eye at all for God.

The other man prayed, "God be merciful to me a sinner." That man may have possessed great wealth, he may have had the courage of a conqueror, but he realized that he lacked something which only God could supply (Luke 18:10,13). The poverty which is a key to God's Kingdom is the realization that, though we possess all things, without God all our things are nothing.

My favorite story is of a boy who had received money from his father, and had a spirit which made him feel he could conquer the world. In spite of his wealth and his spirit, however, he remained poor until one day he fully realized his real poverty, and said, "I will arise and go to my father" (Luke 15:18). There is the poverty that makes rich—the realization of our lack of God and our desire for God.

"Blessed are the poor in spirit: for theirs is the kingdom of heaven." We sometimes interpret that word "blessed" to mean happy, but really it means a oneness with God. The "poor in spirit" have so emptied themselves of themselves—the pride of their accomplishments, the self-ishness of their desires—that the Spirit of God has come into their emptiness. We sing, "What a joy divine, leaning on the everlasting arm"—that is it.

And what do we mean by the kingdom of heaven? Someone has said, "All that religion has to offer is self-denial in this life on the promise of some pie in the sky." But notice that Jesus uses the verb "is." His Kingdom becomes an immediate possession. It is not a place, it is an experience. It is not bounded by geographical lines, it is bounded only by our capacity to receive it.

Possessing the Kingdom, one possesses all things. The children of Israel were terrified. They had put their faith in Moses; he had died, and now they had lost everything. There are those of us today who put our faith in things which can die: rich one moment, we become poverty-stricken the next.

But not Joshua. Listen to his words to these fearful people: "Be strong and of a good courage; be not afraid, neither be thou dismayed; for the Lord thy God is with thee whithersoever thou goest" (Joshua 1:9). Joshua belonged in the kingdom of God.

Possessing God's power enables us to face life with enthusiasm; it gives us a deep inward peace because we are not afraid of tomorrow. There comes into our lives an inner joy that outward circumstances cannot reach. Because God is within us, and because God is love, there flows out from us a love for others that sweeps away all prejudice, jealousy, and hate.

In the light of the blessings of possessing the Kingdom of God, all our other possessions grow so dim that out of our very hearts we sing: "When other helpers fail, and comforts flee, help of the helpless, O abide with me."

2. BLESSED ARE THEY THAT MOURN: FOR THEY SHALL BE COMFORTED

THE SECOND KEY TO THE KINGDOM OF GOD IS MOURNING. That is even less attractive to us than poverty, yet only those who can feel can mourn. There was Father Damien, for thirteen years a missionary to the lepers on Molokai. Finally the dread disease laid hold of him.

One morning he spilled some boiling water on his foot. But there was not the slightest pain. Then he knew he was doomed. He knew that death had come to his body and little by little would take possession. A hundred times better for him would it have been if that boiling water had brought pain.

St. Paul tells us of certain people who were "past feeling" (Ephesians 4:19). That is a horrible condition in which to be, yet, to some extent, each one of us is so afflicted. Socrates described a man's conscience as the wife from whom there is no divorce. Maybe we can't divorce our conscience, but we can stifle it until its voice is completely stilled.

A man whose feet were amputated told of his experience. He was caught out in the bitter cold of the far north. So long as his feet pained him he was happy, but after a while the pain was gone, and he knew then that his feet were doomed. The pain diminished as they froze.

So with conscience. You have committed a certain wrong. Does it hurt? Then be glad. You become hopeless only when your soul becomes past feeling. Stuart N. Hutch-

133

inson tells of a small boy who, having been told by his father that conscience is a small voice which talks to us when we have done wrong, prayed, "O God, make the little voice loud."

"Blessed are they that mourn," said our Lord. He is not talking about the pessimist who constantly looks for the bad, nor of the selfish person whose ambitions have been thwarted, nor of the person who is bitter and rebellious over some loss. The first key to God's Kingdom, "poverty of spirit," tells us we should be conscious of our lack of God. Now, the second key tells us we should be so grieved over our moral and spiritual shortcomings that we cannot rest until we have found God, and our souls are satisfied.

Modern congregations have about discarded the old mourners' bench. It was a place where penitents came seeking divine pardon. In its stead we have a psychological clinic. Certainly I do not disparage the help of modern psychology. I have spent untold hours in counseling, but counseling by itself is not enough.

Today we want God's blessings without the pain of God's purging. We want sermons on how to win friends, how to have peace of mind, and how to forget our fears. But we must remember that Christ came to make men good rather than merely to make men feel good.

Each Sunday night in my own church I give people a chance to come and pray at the altar. An average of between six and seven hundred kneel there. Watching tears streaming down some praying face, I have felt like shouting for joy. The way of the Cross is not easy, but it is the way home.

Jesus told us, "And I, if I be lifted up from the earth,

will draw all men unto me." Then the Gospel record adds, "This he said, signifying what death he should die" (John 12:32,33). And as we see the suffering of the Saviour, surely it must bring suffering to us. Only a dead soul can see Him without mourning.

Let us remember that it is the sins of men that put Him there. If men had traveled less the paths of sin, His path up Calvary would have been less steep. If they had been less greedy and self-seeking, the nails in His hands would have burned less. If they had been less proud, His crown of thorns would have been less painful. If they had loved others more, they would have hated Him less.

On the cross He said, "Father, forgive them; for they know not what they do" (Luke 23:34). Surely Pilate and Caiphas, Herod and the soldiers did not know what they were doing. Greedy, selfish men were merely putting out of the way one who got in their way. Their very ignorance helped Him to bear His cross.

But we do know. We have the record which has been taught to us from childhood. We are the ones who grieve Him most, who make the pain for Him the hardest to bear. He died to heal our broken hearts, and, instead, we break His heart by our own sin and our indifference to Him.

"Blessed are they that mourn." Those who care—care to the point of a broken spirit and a contrite heart, care to a deep repentance.

When Jesus came to Golgotha they hanged Him on a tree;
They drove great nails through hands and feet, and made
    a Calvary;
They crowned Him with a crown of thorns, red were His
    wounds and deep,

For those were crude and cruel days and human flesh was cheap.

When Jesus came to Birmingham, they simply passed Him by,
They never hurt a hair of Him, they only let Him die;
For men had grown more tender, and they would not give Him pain,
They only just passed down the street, and left Him in the rain. (From "The Unutterable Beauty" by G. A. Studdert Kennedy, published by Hodder & Stoughton, Ltd.)

Maybe you are afraid. You dread to come into His presence. You are ashamed to face Him. You may feel miserable inside. Then take heart and be glad, for your very shame and misery and fear are a mourning that can lead you to His comfort.

As you look at your life you may see your own broken heart. Be glad that it is broken. Take it to Calvary. There, under the warm glow of His love, your broken heart can be welded together again, and your sorrow be turned into rejoicing. Be thankful for your broken heart, if by becoming broken we are led to Christ for the mending.

3. BLESSED ARE THE MEEK: FOR THEY SHALL INHERIT THE EARTH

ONE OF THE KEYS TO THE KINGDOM OF GOD IS MEEKNESS. But we do not want to be meek. We prefer to be like the little boy whose mother kept calling him, "My little lamb." Finally, he said, "Mother, I don't want to be your little lamb. I want to be your little tiger."

We like to think of ourselves as being courageous and strong. We sing with inspiration, "The Son of God goes forth to war, a kingly crown to gain," but meekness does not appeal to us. We want to be conquerors, and meekness sounds too much like surrender. Meekness does mean surrender, but not surrender to men around us, not surrender to ourselves, not surrender to the circumstances of our lives.

For the true meaning of meekness turn to the Thirty-seventh Psalm. There you find it stated, "The meek shall inherit the earth." The Hebrew word which is translated "meek" really means "to be molded." The Psalmist says, 'Fret not thyself because of evil-doers," do not be envious of the prosperity of the wicked. Instead, "Commit thy way unto the Lord." That is, let yourself become as putty in God's hand, be molded by Him, yield your life to the purposes of God, and eventually real success will be your reward.

Jesus lifted up that phrase of the Psalmist and made it one of the Beatitudes, a key to God's Kingdom. The New Testament writers used the Greek word *praos*, which we translate as "meek." Actually, it means to be controlled. It means submission to the divine plan of God.

The laws of God are already established when we are born. His ways are fixed. We have a choice in that we can accept God's way and live according to His law, or we can rebel against Him. But we cannot change what He has done. For example, the world is round and the sky is blue. Suppose you don't like round worlds and blue skies. There is nothing you can do about it.

Also did God make the laws of the universe, which are just as unchangeable as is the universe itself. There are the seasons. The farmer learns the laws of the seasons and becomes governed by them. He plants his crop when it should be planted and thus he reaps when he should be reaping. For him to rebel and plant out of season does not change the laws of God, it means only the failure of his crop. For the farmer meekness means planting when he should plant. It means submission to God's laws.

So with life. God has His will, and man has his will. Man has the choice of being meek or of being self-willed. He can say with Christ, "Nevertheless, not my will, but thine, be done" (Luke 22:42), or man can say, "I will do as I please." The Psalmist says, "Delight thyself also in the Lord; and he shall give thee the desires of thine heart." (Psalm 37:4). On the other hand, to fail to become molded or controlled by God's will is to destroy ourselves.

In the last chapter of the book of Job is a thrilling statement. Job's life had both sunshine and shadows. He had his successes and also his defeats. He had faith in God, yet there were times of doubt. It seemed that Job might "curse God," as he was advised to do. But in the end his faith triumphs and Job says, "I know that thou canst do everything" (42:2).

There are times when, with our limited vision, it seems that God's way is not the best way. We want material success on earth, we want happiness in our lives and peace in our hearts. If we believed, really believed, God would give us what we so much want; we would gladly be meek, that is, be willing to be molded and controlled by God. But it wasn't until he became an old man that Job knew without doubt that God is never defeated.

How wonderful it is to learn that lesson while there is still much of life to be lived. One of the sublimest statements outside the Bible comes from Dante, "In His will is our peace." The opposite of peace is conflict and the reason we do not have peace of mind and soul is that we are at war within ourselves.

There is the voice of duty and there is the voice of inclination, both within us demanding to be heard. We struggle to decide, and the struggle squanders our powers. We become weakened and exhausted. But when one decides to do the will of God, day by day, as best he understands it, the conflict is resolved.

Such a decision takes all of the dread out of tomorrow. The wise man of the Bible tells us, "In all thy ways acknowledge him, and he shall direct thy paths" (Proverbs 3:6). The very act of accepting the will of God for your life today places the responsibility of what happens tomorrow on God. So we do not worry about what the result will be. There is wonderful peace in leaving the results in His hands. An old Negro man once prayed, "When God tells me to butt my head against a rock wall it's my place to butt. It's the Lord's place to go through." As you study the lives of God-molded people down through the centuries you realize that every time God did "go through." In the long run, God is never defeated.

I think of how Mahatma Gandhi left Sabarmati on March 12, 1930, to go on the "salt march." He proposed to march to the sea, there make salt, which was a government monopoly, and thus precipitate a crisis. He said he would not return until he had gained independence for India.

It seemed absurd. A little man in a loin cloth and with a bamboo walking stick going out to do battle against the greatest empire the world had ever known. But seventeen years later the little man had won. Gandhi's power lay in the fact that his life was committed to the will of God as he understood it. Thus committed, he was totally without fear. And his/freedom from fear struck fear into the heart of the British Empire and it dared not destroy him.

"Blessed are the meek," said Jesus. Those who surrender to God possess God. We are told, "The earth is the Lord's and the fulness thereof" (Psalm 24:1). Thus, possessing God, the meek do also "inherit the earth."

4. BLESSED ARE THEY WHICH DO HUNGER AND THIRST AFTER RIGHTEOUSNESS: FOR THEY SHALL BE FILLED

ONCE A YOUNG MAN CAME TO BUDDHA SEEKING THE TRUE way of life, the path of deliverance. According to the story as Dr. Ralph Sockman tells it, Buddha led him down to the river. The young man assumed that he was to undergo some ritual of purification, some type of baptismal service.

They walked out into the river for some distance and suddenly Buddha grabbed the man and held his head under the water. Finally, in a last gasp, the fellow wrenched himself lose, and his head came above the water. Quietly Buddha asked him, "When you thought you were drowning, what did you desire most?" The man gasped, "Air." Back came Buddha's reply, "When you want salvation as much as you wanted air, then you will get it."

Jesus would agree with that. He tells us that one of the keys to the Kingdom of God is to hunger and thirst for it. We get what we really want. The poet Shelley pointed out that imagination is the great instrument of moral good. When the imagination and the will are in conflict the imagination always wins.

To imagine is to form mental images on the screen of our minds. It means to create in our thinking what we want created in our living. One's time, talents, and all other resources become organized and dedicated to the purpose of making real the objects of his imagination. As Georgia Harkness said, "Be careful what you set your heart on, for you will surely get it."

Jesus tells us that before we can possess God and the things of God we must first make God the center of our imagination. "Thou shalt love the Lord thy God with all thy heart, and with all thy soul, and with all thy mind" (Matthew 22:37), said Christ. And when God becomes the very center of our affection, our feeling, and our thinking, we shall find and possess and be possessed by God.

The greatest thrill this preacher ever has is to see some person attain a deeper experience of God. Every Sunday night, as I see hundreds pray at the altar of the church, I know that some are finding God there. But long before time for the altar prayers I can almost pick out those who will be blessed that night.

Watch a congregation during the organ prelude and you will see a lot of difference. Some are quiet in thought and prayer. They seem hardly conscious of their immediate surroundings. Others are chatting away with everyone around, they watch others as they come in, note their clothes, and wonder about them.

When the hymn is announced, some sing not only with their voices but also with their hearts. Others just say the words or don't even bother to pick up the hymn-book. During the sermon some are like blotters. They soak up every thought and mood of the preacher. Others seem utterly unresponsive.

What makes the difference? Some have needs that human resources do not supply. They have come to church feeling that need, hungering and thirsting for God, and it is they who find Him. You never find God until He becomes your deepest desire.

Two men were discussing New York City. One said it was a wicked place, filled with cheap sensations, with morally degraded people, with sin on every corner. The other said it is a grand place, filled with art museums, great music, and stimulating lectures. New York was the city that each inwardly desired.

We find in life what we want to find. So Jesus said, "Blessed are they which do hunger and thirst after right-eousness: for they shall be filled."

It bothers me that the church seems to mean so little to many of its members, that in the church so many find almost no help. It is not the church, it is our own attitudes. Once a rather pious churchman was reproving his neighbor for profanity. The profane neighbor replied, "Well, my friend, I cuss a lot and you pray a lot, but neither of us really means what he says."

In one of his books Bishop Fulton J. Sheen says, "It is not uncommon to find Catholics who say: 'I knew I should not eat meat on Friday out of respect for the day on which Our Lord sacrificed His life for me, but I did not want to embarrass my host,' or, 'I was staying with some unbelieving friends over the week end and I did not want to embarrass them, so I did not go to Mass on Sunday'. . . . Such is the indifference of the world, a fear of being identified whole-heartedly with God, for whom we were made."

What he says of Catholics is, perhaps, even more true of Protestants. If we really desire God we will do those things which will cause us to experience God. Jesus says that we should hunger and thirst after God. I saw a picture show recently of a man lost on the hot sands of a desert, without water. His thirst whipped his weary body to the point of madness. His distorted mind was mocked with a cruel mirage of an oasis. He died frantically digging with his bare hands in the sand.

"Thirst" is a strong word, a driving word. And when the human soul thirsts for God, Jesus says he will be filled with God. And not only will we find God for ourselves, we will bring God's Kingdom on earth.

Just suppose that there was only one real believer on earth and that during an entire year this one believer made one convert. Then there would be two. Suppose that during the next year these two made one convert apiece, then there would be four. Suppose that the next year these four made one convert apiece, then there would be eight. Suppose that they kept that pace of each winning one every year, how long would it take to convert every person in the entire world?

It has now been two thousand years since our Lord was on earth. Has that been enough time? Actually, there has been time enough, with just one winning one other per year, to convert sixty-five worlds like this. Starting with just one and doubling each year, at the end of just thirty-one years there would be 2,147,483,648 souls filled with God's righteousness. The next year they could convert another world the size of this one.

We can have God in our souls and in our world whenever we really want Him.

5. BLESSED ARE THE MERCIFUL: FOR THEY SHALL OBTAIN MERCY

OF THE EIGHT BEATITUDES, THE KEYS TO GOD'S KINGDOM, this one is the most appealing, the most important, and the most difficult. Most appealing because mercy brings to mind kindness, unselfish service, and good will. Everyone loves the Good Samaritan and Florence Nightingale, who are examples of mercy. We shrink from the justice of God, but we pray for His mercy.

Most important, for without mercy all of us are without hope. All of us have sinned and come short of God's glory. The only prayer we can pray is, "God be merciful to me a sinner" (Luke 18:13). As Portia said to Shylock, "In the course of justice none of us should see salvation."

When we come to the Communion table we pray, "We are not worthy so much as to gather up the crumbs under Thy table. But Thou art the same Lord whose property is always to have mercy." However, the key to God's mercy toward ourselves is the mercy we have toward others. If we are not merciful, then we are blocking God's mercy out of our own lives, and thus we become doomed men and women.

There is a saying, "All that goes up must come down," but if nothing goes up, then nothing will come down. In physics we are taught that every action has a reaction, but if there is no action, then there can be no reaction. "If ye forgive not men their trespasses, neither will your Father forgive your trespasses" (Matthew 6:15). Without forgiving, forgiveness cannot be obtained. Be merciful, and ye shall obtain mercy.

The most expensive thing you can do is hold a wrong spirit in your heart against another. The price you pay is the loss, the eternal loss, of your own soul. In talking about the Kingdom of Heaven Jesus tells the story of a king who forgave his servant a large debt which he could not pay. That same servant met a fellow servant who owed him a trifling sum, and because he could not pay, the poor fellow was thrown into prison by the unmerciful servant. The king called back the servant whom he had forgiven, cancelled his forgiveness, and had him cast into prison.

Jesus concludes the story, "So likewise shall my heavenly Father do also unto you, if ye from your hearts forgive not every one his brother their trespasses" (Matthew 18:23-35).

Protestants do not regard Peter as the head of the Church as do Catholics, yet beautiful is the explanation a Catholic friend gave to me of why he believes Peter was chosen. James and John asked for the chief places, but they were passed by, as was the Virgin Mother, or one of the others. Peter was chosen because he sinned so shamefully but later wept so bitterly. Tradition tells us that Peter wept so much that even his cheeks became furrowed with tears.

So the Lord chose him who knew by experience the blessing of merciful forgiveness in order that his life should cause the Church to put at its very center mercy toward others, thereby saving itself as it saved others. Without being merciful, no one can enter the Kingdom of God. Not only is this key the most appealing and important, also it is the most difficult. When someone has done us wrong our natural human reaction is to seek revenge, to get even. We might refuse to commit any definite act of vengeance, yet cherish resentment and be glad if some misfortune happened to him.

Mercy requires not only a right spirit on our part against a person who has wronged us, not only that we must overcome all vindictiveness, jealousy, and littleness, but that we must do even more than feel a kind spirit in our hearts. Jesus wept, but He did more than weep. He gave Himself even unto death to serve and save those who had persecuted Him.

In his book, *High Wind At Noon*, Allan Knight Chalmers gives us the story of Peer Holm, who was a world-famous engineer. He built great bridges, railroads and tunnels in many parts of the earth; he gained wealth and fame, but later came to failure, poverty, and sickness. He returned to the little village where he was born and, together with his wife and little girl, eked out a meager living.

Peer Holm had a neighbor who owned a fierce dog. Peer warned him that the dog was dangerous, but the old man contemptuously replied, "Hold your tongue, you cursed pauper." One day Peer Holm came home to find the dog at the throat of his little girl. He tore the dog away, but the dog's teeth had gone too deeply and the little girl was dead.

The sheriff shot the dog, and the neighbors were bitter against his owner. When sowing time came they refused to sell him any grain. His fields were plowed but bare. He could neither beg, borrow, nor buy seed. Whenever he walked down the road, the people of the village sneered at him. But not Peer Holm. He could not sleep at night for thinking of his neighbor.

Very early one morning he rose, went to his shed, and got his last half bushel of barley. He climbed the fence and sowed his neighbor's field. The fields themselves told the story. When the seeds came up, it was revealed what Peer had done, because part of his own field remained bare while the field of his neighbor was green.

Mercy requires that we sow good seed in our enemy's field, even though it means that part of our own field will be left bare. It is not easy. It is the hardest possible action, but it is our key to God's Kingdom.

The way of the world was an eye for an eye and a tooth for a tooth. Hate always led to hate. Wrong always brought revenge. But one day the vicious circle was broken. One called Jesus came offering men a higher way and a better iife, but men stood back to mock and to laugh and to crucify.

About His head was a bright circle, and when He uttered the word, "Forgive," that circle of God's love and approval became large enough to include others. A thief on a cross near by stepped inside that circle with Him and in so doing entered Paradise. The circle reaches to my own feet. To stay outside is to know hate, revenge, and destruction. Inside is to know God's healing love and eternally to possess His Kingdom.

The step into the circle is the step to mercy. "Blessed are the merciful: for they shall obtain mercy."

6. BLESSED ARE THE PURE IN HEART: FOR THEY SHALL SEE GOD

THERE ARE MANY THINGS I WOULD LIKE TO SEE—THE GRAND Canyon, some of the great cathedrals of Europe, the paths in the Holy Land along which the Saviour walked. I want to continue to see my home happy and peaceful, I want to see my children growing mentally and spiritually as well as physically, and some day become established in some useful work in the world. I want to see always the difference between right and wrong. Most of all, I want to see God.

But all people have not the same ability to see. Many people have limited vision. Some are cross-eyed, the eyes of some are weak and diseased. Some people have a growth called a cataract, which shuts off vision. Some are near-sighted, others, far-sighted; some are color-blind, others have blind spots in their eyes. Sidney Lanier looked at the muddy, crooked Chattahoochee river and saw in it a lovely poem; Joel Chandler Harris saw in rabbits, foxes, 'possums, and an old man named Uncle Remus, stories which will live forever. Woodrow Wilson could see a basis of lasting world peace, but tragically so few others saw it. Sir Christopher Wren could see a beautiful cathedral and make of that vision a temple to God.

There are at least three ways in which we see. St. Paul tells us that "eye hath not seen, nor ear heard, neither have entered into the heart of man, the things which God hath prepared for them that love him" (I Corinthians 2:9). There we have pointed out three kinds of sight. There is the sight of the natural eye, with which we can see flowers and mountains, the printed words on this page, and people's faces. That is physical vision.

A teacher may explain to a boy a problem in mathematics or chemistry. As the teacher talks, the boy hears, and his mind takes hold of what he hears to the point of understanding. After he understands, he may say, "I see it." That is mental sight. In studying botany a student can reach the point of learning the various kinds of flowers and of their culture and development. Then he can see flowers with both his physical and mental eyes. If one understands what he reads, he sees with both his eyes and his mind.

But there is still a third sight, as when a truth has "entered into the heart of man." The heart has eyes, too. Robert Burns saw in flowers thoughts too deep for tears. Not only did he see flowers with his physical eyes, not only did he understand the growth and culture of flowers, also he felt their message. Jesus looked at people and had "compassion on them."

He saw them not only with His eyes and mind, but also with His heart. One can read the Twenty-third Psalm and understand the meaning of the words and phrases. But some read it and they feel the message and know the Good Shepherd. A boy can look at a girl and know that he loves her. He sees her not only with his eyes but with his heart.

A person sees God through the eyes of the heart. "Blessed are the pure in heart: for they shall see God" (Matthew 5:8). Jesus said: "He that hath seen me hath seen the Father" (John 14:9). Certainly not every person who saw Him with his physical eyes saw God. Mere physical sight of Him revealed only a man. It is not even enough to understand His teachings and His life. Many scholars have studied His words without seeing Him. Really to see God in Christ one must experience Him in the heart.

What a wonderful change in my life has been wrought,
Since Jesus came into my heart.
I have light in my soul for which long I have sought,
Since Jesus came into my heart.

When the heart sees Christ, then we see God. To see God is to realize Him, to feel Him, to center the affections of the heart in Him.

But one can have an indistinct and distorted picture of God. Read the story, "The Quest for the Holy Grail." The holy grail was the mystic cup used at the Last Supper, in which legend has it that Joseph of Arimathea caught the last drop of blood which fell from our Lord's side as He died on the cross. Sir Galahad, along with other Knights of the Round Table, set out in quest of it. In the story

150

they found it, but each saw it through the mirror of his own soul.

To some it was swathed in mist and cloud. Their vision was very indistinct. Sir Lancelot saw it, but his heart was a sinful heart. He saw the holy grail covered with holy wrath and fire. To him it was a vision of stern and awful retribution. Sir Galahad also saw the grail. He was the knight with the white soul. Of him it was said, "His strength was the strength of ten because his heart was pure." For him the vision was clear and radiant and glorious.

How we see God depends on the condition of our hearts. To some He is a cloudy mystery, to others He is awful punishment, but to the pure in heart He is a friend and a glorious certainty.

Suppose one has lost purity of heart, can it be re-gained? Can a harlot become a virgin again? Yes, St. Augustine refers to Mary Magdalene as "the arch-virgin." Not content to call her merely a pure woman, he lifts her far above other women. She was a common prostitute of the streets. She was both vile and vulgar. But one day she came in contact with Him who was the purest. She so loved Him with her heart that all her affection was poured out on Him. She so completely took Him to heart that her evil desires were cast out. Being filled with the purity of Christ, she herself became pure.

In just a little while we see her standing at the foot of Jesus' cross. See who is by her side! It is Mary, the Lord's mother, the blessed Virgin. The two are standing together. Purity has been regained. Paradise lost has now been regained. And on Easter morning Mary Magdalene became the first vessel chosen by Christ Himself in which to send forth the blessed Gospel. If Mary Magdalene could become pure again, then there is hope for every one of us. She saw Christ with her heart.

"Blessed are the pure in heart: for they shall see God."

7. BLESSED ARE THE PEACEMAKERS: FOR THEY SHALL BE CALLED THE CHILDREN OF GOD

WHAT DO WE WANT MOST OF ALL? WHENEVER I AM IN THE vicinity of Warm Springs, I like to stop by the little cottage which Franklin D. Roosevelt loved so much. There he would come to rest and to think in the quietness of that lovely place. The night before he died he was there planning a trip to San Francisco to attend the organization of the United Nations. He was writing his speech—the last words he ever wrote. They were:

We seek peace—enduring peace. . . . We must cultivate the science of human relations—the ability of all peoples, of all kinds, to live together and work together, in the same world, at peace. . . . As we go forward toward the greatest contribution that any generation of human beings can make in the world—the contribution of lasting peace— I ask you to keep up your faith.

Above all things, peace was the desire of his heart, as it is of my heart and of yours. We want peace in our world—we want peace inside ourselves. The fact that the late Rabbi Joshua Loth Liebman's book *Peace of Mind* has now sold nearly a million copies is eloquent testimony that people are interested in peace.

The angel climaxed the announcement of the birth of our Lord with the words, "Glory to God in the highest, and on earth peace, good will toward men" (Luke 2:14). Peace was His mission. "Peace I leave with you, my peace I give unto you" (John 14:27). When we think of the Kingdom of God, we think of a kingdom of peace, where all strife has ceased. So we are not surprised that our Lord gave peace as one of the keys to the Kingdom.

As Rabbi Liebman pointed out at the beginning of his book, there are many earthly things we desire—health, love, riches, beauty, talent, power, fame; but without peace of mind all those things bring torment instead of joy. If we have peace, no matter what else we may lack, life is worth living. Without peace, though we may possess all things else, it is not enough.

What is peace? The mere absence of strife is not peace. At the moment Jesus was speaking of peace there was no war on earth, but neither was there peace. The Roman Empire had forced the world to its knees and the people had lost both the means and the will to fight. When Paris surrendered to the German fury without a struggle, someone said, "London lost her buildings, but Paris lost her soul."

Peace is a positive force. You may clear some plot of land of every noxious weed, but that will not make of it a garden. It will be only a barren field. It becomes a garden when flowers are growing there. The prophet of old reminds us that just to break up our swords and spears is not enough. Those swords must become plowshares and the spears pruning hooks (Micah 4:3).

To have peace in both the world and our souls, not only must hate, suspicion and fear be rooted out. Also must love, joy, patience and understanding be planted and cultivated. Peace is something to be made; thus we must be peacemakers if we are to enter the kingdom of God.

The place to begin making peace is within ourselves. Dr. Ralph W. Sockman in his book, *The Higher Happiness*, which is the most helpful book on the Beatitudes I know, lifts up the words of Christ, "And if a house be divided against itself, that house cannot stand" (Mark 3:25). Then he points out three ways by which a life is divided: between its inner self and its outer self, between its forward drive and its backward pull, between its higher and lower natures. Let's look at these a moment.

Inner and Outer Selves. The Pharisees became chiefly concerned with keeping up a front. All of their actions were "to be seen of men." They were worried about what the neighbors would think. Seeking to appear to be something outside which they were not inside, they became hypocrites. A hypocrite is one without peace. Unless our outward appearances and our inward character are in harmony with each other, we have no peace.

Forward and Backward. Physically, we are made to go forward. To walk backward is awkward. A little girl was trying to button her dress in the back. Finally, she gave up and went to her mother for help, saying, "I can't do it because I am in front of myself." But mentally we are just the opposite. We can think better backward than forward. We know what happened yesterday, we can only guess about tomorrow. Thus it is easier to live in the past, and reluctantly we turn it loose.

We load ourselves down with the futile regrets and mistakes of yesterday; thus the business of living becomes a hard pull. Instead of repentance, we know only the meaning of remorse. Remorse is futile worry and self-inflicted agony for some yesterday. Repentance is a redemptive experience which leads to forgiveness. It buries the past under the blessed hope of tomorrow.

Higher and Lower Natures. Finally, we make peace by the decisions of our souls. Elijah stood before the people on Mount Carmel and pleaded, "How long halt ye between two opinions? If the Lord be God, follow him: but if Baal, then follow him." He was pleading for a decision. The Bible says, "And the people answered him not a word" (I Kings 18:21). Oh, the tragedy of one who cannot make a decision. There is marvelous inner peace which comes to one who completely decides for God. I suppose there is a peace, certainly a cessation of inner strife, which comes to one who decides against God. But to go through life undecided is to live in misery. "No man can serve two masters." Two thousand years ago Jesus said that, yet we have not learned it.

The oldest story of man tells how he sinned and then hid himself from God. Hiding from God is the most miserable experience the human soul can experience. Peace with God is the most blessed experience. One of the greatest thinkers of all time was Copernicus. He revolutionized the thinking of mankind in regard to the universe. The epitaph on his grave at Frauenburg is this: "I do not seek a kindness equal to that given to Paul; nor do I ask the grace granted to Peter; but that forgiveness which thou didst give to the robber—that I earnestly pray." That is the way to begin making peace.

The angel said, "Glory to God," before he said, "Peace on earth."

8. BLESSED ARE THEY WHICH ARE PERSE-CUTED FOR RIGHTEOUSNESS' SAKE: FOR THEIRS IS THE KINGDOM OF HEAVEN

THE SERMON ON THE MOUNT RECORDED IN MATTHEW 5, 6, and 7 is really the pattern of the Kingdom of God on earth. Jesus begins that sermon with the listing of the eight keys to that kingdom, the qualities of character of the Godly person. The climax of the Beatitudes and the sermon are really one and the same.

In the sermon He tells us how to live, and He concludes with a call to action, the expression of those principles in daily living. "Whosoever heareth these sayings of mine, *and doeth them*," He says. At the beginning of the sermon He lists the qualities of character, as poverty of spirit, mourning, meekness, desire for righteousness, mercy, purity of heart, and peacemaking. Then He says, "Blessed are they which are persecuted." That is, actually to live these keys to the kingdom will cost something. But unless they are translated into life they are worthless.

Jesus never promised ease to those who follow Him. Never did He put a carpet on the race track or a bed of roses on the battlefield. He talked about self-denial, about crosses, blood-spattered, death-dealing crosses. To enter the Kingdom of God may mean decisions that are hard, consecration that leads to persecution. But it can be no other way.

In Revelation, St. John writes to the Christians, "Fear none of those things which thou shalt suffer: behold, the devil shall cast some of you into prison, that ye may be tried; and ye shall have tribulation ten days [indefinitely]: be thou faithful unto death, and I will give thee a crown of life" (2:10). Notice carefully one little word there. He does not say "until" death, but "unto" death. That means, be faithful, not merely until you die, but even though it kills you. Make whatever sacrifice is required, even die, before you be unfaithful.

A minister friend tells of going to a large church to preach at a special Good Friday night service. The weather was extremely bad and only a few people came. Apologetically, the pastor said to the visiting minister, "If it had not been for the bad weather we would have had a large crowd to hear you tonight."

At first, it angered the visiting minister, but quickly his anger turned to pity and contempt. Looking at his host, he said, "Do you realize what you have just said? If the weather had not been bad a larger crowd would have come to this Good Friday service. Jesus died on Good Friday, but His followers did not come to the service because the weather was bad."

When I started in the ministry I did not have a car. Sometimes I would walk to my little churches, sometimes I would borrow the horse and buggy of an old physician, Dr. George Burnett. One very cold and rainy Sunday morning I said to the doctor that I would not go to the little church out in the country because I doubted that anyone would be there. He looked at me with contempt. I will never forget the sternness of his voice. He said, "It is your duty to be there. Get the horse and go."

No person ever really lives until he has found something worth dying for. You can never really possess the Kingdom of God until the cause of God becomes more important than your own life.

William L. Stidger told about a young lad he had baptized as a baby. The boy grew up, and when World War II began, he joined the Navy. One night his ship came into Boston, and the lad visited his former pastor and friend. During their visit together, Dr. Stidger said, "Bill, tell me the most exciting experience you have had thus far." The boy seemed to hesitate. It wasn't that he had difficulty in selecting the most exciting experience. Rather, the experience he had in mind was so wonderful and sacred that he had difficulty in putting it into words.

He was the captain of a large transport and, along with a big convoy, was making his way across the Atlantic. One day an enemy submarine rose in the sea close by. He saw the white mark of the torpedo coming directly toward his transport, loaded with hundreds of boys. He had no time to change course. Through the loud-speaker he shouted, "Boys, this is it!"

Near by was a little escorting destroyer. The captain of that destroyer also saw the submarine and the torpedo. Without a moment's hesitation, he gave the order, "Full speed ahead." Into the path of the torpedo the tiny destroyer went and took the full impact of the deadly missile midship. The destroyer was blown apart, quickly it sank, and every man of the crew was lost.

For a long time the boy remained silent. Then he looked at his beloved pastor and said, "Dr. Stidger, the skipper of that destroyer was my best friend." Again he was quiet for a while, then slowly he said: "You know there is a verse in the Bible which has special meaning for me now. It is, "Greater love hath no man than this, that a man lay down his life for his friends" (John 15:13).

> *The Son of God goes forth to war,*
> *A kingly crown to gain.*
> *His blood-red banner streams afar;*
> *Who follows in His train?*

To be poor in spirit means to give up our pride; to mourn means to be penitent to the point of surrendering our sins; meekness means that we must surrender our very selves to the plans and purposes of God; our hunger for God means turning away from our ambitions for all things else; to be merciful means to pay good for the evil we have received; for purity we must give up all things impure; to make peace is wholly to choose God. Those are the seven ingredients of righteousness. They must be bought at a price. Blessed are those who pay the price, "for theirs is the kingdom of God."